Memoir on Two Wheels

Foreword

I have had a lifelong love affair with cycling!

It all started when I was in the 2nd year (Year 8) at my secondary school in Coventry. And you've guessed .... It was all because of a boy.

He was tall, with mousy coloured hair and he was into cycling. One of the tasks we had to do at school in the second year (Year 8) was give a talk to the rest of the class about a hobby we were passionate about. I can't remember what my subject was but it might have been about philately – stamp collecting. This boy's talk was about his summer holiday with 3 friends cycling and youth hostelling from Coventry to Swanage. Having an absolute teenage crush on this boy, I was all 'ears' as he described his adventure.

That was it. I would take up cycling to get myself noticed by him.

I used to cycle to school on my Grandmother's 28-year old Armstrong sit-up-and-beg roadster. All the boys had sports bikes with weird chains that wrapped around small cogwheels at the back wheel and a big wheel by the pedals .... I later discovered these were derailleur gears. There was I, trying to keep up with these boys – and this tall one in particular – as we came out of school. I used to put my hands on the brake levers instead of the handlebars to give myself a more streamlined position, similar to being on dropped handlebars. How dangerous was that!

If that were all I had to do to make an impression on Heartthrob, I would have cracked it. BUT .... There was one insurmountable obstacle in the shape of an attractive, willowy blonde who was already his girlfriend.

Being short and wearing glasses, I stood no chance!! My teenage crush was a non-starter.

However, I enjoyed my cycle rides to school and also went

out for cycling picnics with my friends in the school holidays and, even though I'd given up making any headway with my 'Heartthrob', I often thought about the talk he gave at school and the adventure he had cycling to Swanage.

Contents

Chapter 1 – Family Dedication

I am writing this book for my family so they understand a bit more about this crazy Mother and Grandmother. This is for my two sons and all my grandchildren. At the time of writing I have six grandchildren … so I'm leaving my options open in case any more come along!

Whilst living in Huddersfield towards the end of 1980, Andy Thompson (my husband at the time) and I became aware that we would become parents and had the pregnancy confirmed. Growth progressed and my body grew as expected. However, after a while the medical profession suggested I check my dates as I was larger than expected. I thought I was most likely carrying a lot of water in my womb.

After about 12 weeks I had a scan and all appeared to be in order other than when I noticed the staff giving each other 'looks' and I thought no more of it. About half way through my pregnancy I had another scan and was very grateful that I was lying down as I was told I was expecting twins!! You can imagine the surprise when I told Andy when I got back.

Alex Ross Thompson was born at 11.03 pm and Vincent Sebastian Thompson was born at 11.05 pm on 6 June 1981 by Caesarean section as they got tangled in my womb. They were both fit and healthy with Alex weighing in a 5 lbs 9 oz and Vincent at 6 lbs 4 oz. Good sizes – no wonder I was so huge.

In the hospital, I finally came around from all the anaesthetic and was confused to see a different coloured set of curtains around my bed. What happened next completely threw me. As a nurse drew away my curtains, there was a **MAN** in the bed opposite. I was in a maternity ward!!!? Apparently, I had taken so long to come round from the anaesthetic after the Caesarean section, I had been put into Intensive Care!

In 1983 we moved back to the Midlands and Andy set up Orbit Cycles in Dudley where he worked until 1988 and I had some part-time jobs whilst also looking after Alex and Vincent. In 1989 Andy and I parted and eventually divorced in 1991, which was a great upheaval for all concerned and Alex and Vincent in particular.

Throughout all these difficult years being able to ride my bike helped to keep my sanity. Just to get out into the local countryside, often on my own, was such a gift and enabled me to appreciate nature and my local environment. As the boys grew older, I was able to go out cycling with them and also on club runs with my cycling club, it gave me the social interaction I needed.

By the time Alex and Vincent were teenagers and had finished their schooling, I was able to get more adventurous with my bike rides and in 2001 I took a cycling holiday to Northern France using the Sea Cat from Poole to St Malo. On this ship I met Steve Glennie-Smith – also on his way for a solo cycling holiday. It turned out we were staying at the same Youth Hostel and after sharing an evening meal, we set off in the same direction the following morning until I realised I had another 40 miles to ride and it was already mid-day. Thankfully we had swapped contact details before we parted. Over the ensuing months Steve and I kept in touch by email and about 8 months later he came to stay with me and ride along the lanes near where I live. That was the start of a friendship that became so much more and we are still together now although we are both fiercely independent and choose to live apart.

Andy married Malanda Wisdom in 2004 and both are very happy with a menagerie of animals and rescue greyhounds.

Despite the differences we suffered following the divorce, there is now an amicable and supportive relationship between Andy and I and with Malanda and Steve so that we can all be there for Alex and Vincent and their families.

Vincent and Jade brought Ruby into the world in 2007, then came Molly in 2009. Then came Charlie in 2012. Alex and Gemma

2

married in 2011 and Elsa was born in 2013 (named after the lion, not the character from Frozen). In 2017 Finley arrived for Alex and Gemma and, as of the time of writing, Bella was born in 2019 to Vincent and Jude, as he was then separated from Jade.

All the grandchildren bring me so much joy and I love being able to watch them grow and learn about their interests.

I have a brother, Christopher Gordon-Smith and sister Patricia Gordon-Smith who both live in London with their families.

Chapter 2 – Cycling Clubs

When I was 15 my family moved from Coventry to Evesham and this is where my life of cycling really began as I joined the Evesham & District Wheelers Cycling Club, thanks to Gordon Taylor who ran the local bike shop and was an active member of the Evesham club. Here I was introduced to club runs, touring and racing.

Clubruns were the basics of my growing expertise with cycling – voyages of discovery around my local area and increasing my deep love of nature and the countryside.

I distinctly remember my first club run – it was from Evesham to Upton-on-Severn – a fairly easy ride along quiet, flat roads and was about 35 miles long. Feeling confident I could keep up 'with the lads', I went out with them again a few weeks later to Bourton-on-the-Water. That was a different kettle of fish, climbing the Cotswold Hills!

Soon, my clubmates started time trial racing and kept persuading me to 'have a go'. This is when riders are set off at 1-minute intervals and the winner is the person who records the fastest time. So, on 22 May 1968, I rode my first 10-mile time trial, using my Dawes Diamond open-framed bicycle, having taken my mudguards off to save weight. My time was 31 minutes and 8 seconds and, apparently that wasn't bad for a first attempt.

Each year cycling clubs hold an annual dinner and prize presentation and at one such event I experienced a very embarrassing moment during the traditional 'cross-toasting' shenanigans in which my club-mates loved to tease each other. One of them asked 'I'd like to take wine with all the lady members who are in the club'. I proudly stood up amidst huge guffaws of laughter. It was two weeks later on a clubrun that one of my club-mates explained what had been so funny about being 'in the club'!

My cycling confidence grew over time, building on my club runs experience, going on longer rides and relishing in the fact that I was the only girl within the group of lads. Soon I began to enter 'Open' time trial races and competed against other women. One of my highlights was going to a local race where Beryl Burton was racing and watching my 'idol' compete for the first time.

My parents moved to Stourbridge in 1970 but I loved the life I was leading at Evesham so much that I took some lodgings in Sedgeberrow, near Evesham – the village where my family had lived for 3 years. When that didn't work out, I was very grateful when Kate and Roy Packwood took me in at their home near Pershore so I could continue living in the area and also continue cycle racing as they were also members of the Evesham & District Wheelers. Both had supported some of the leading riders from the Midlands Cycle & Athletic Club in the 1950's and 1960's. Roy helped me a lot building my confidence and creating training programmes and taking me to races, always supported by Kate. Kate was like a second Mum to me and we were very close right up until she died in 2011.

Although I am grateful for the belief Roy had in me, this became bittersweet when he began to take liberties with me, so I walked away from them both until after he died in 1972. I carried the scars of Roy's deceit for many years. At the time I was lodging with the Packwoods, I had been seeing a young man who was my first love. However, my passion for cycling and the possibility that I could be successful at racing overtook my heart, so I believed Roy when he told me I needed to give 100% effort to my racing and not have the distraction of a boyfriend. I felt sad for many weeks and threw myself even more into my training, which began to give me favourable results. Roy then started making protestations of affections towards me, which I shunned at every opportunity – he was more than old enough to be my father! It took 10 years for the penny to drop on my naïve mind that Roy had persuaded me to break off with my boyfriend for his own gratification. Definitely a case of 'Me Too'. I never gave him that satisfaction and have been full or remorse for the way I treated the boyfriend at the time.

After trying to become a PE Teacher at college in Bromsgrove, I left feeling disillusioned and moved back with my parents in Stourbridge in 1971. It was no longer practical for me to ride for the Evesham & District Wheelers cycling club so I joined the Beacon Roads Cycling club, based in Northfield, South Birmingham. Christine and Rod Goodfellow were members and we were soon joined by June Pitchford, a prolific 'second in command' to Beryl Burton and also Janet Crowther – both had competed in World Championships in the 1960's. Chris and husband Rod invited me to ride my first road race at Highley, Shropshire in 1971 and I realised I hadn't got a clue how to compete at this discipline.

Many a time I met Chris and Rod so we could ride together to the clubroom from the outskirts of Stourbridge to Longbridge, Birmingham. They had already ridden 18 miles or so from Highley in Shropshire along a very hilly route and it was as much as I could do to keep up with the relentless pace they set the rest of the way to Northfield.

Chris, June, Janet and I set several Road Time Trials Council (RTTC) team records at several time trial distances and were often in the highest 10 women riders in the Best All-rounder competition each year. Chris, in particular did a lot to help me progress in my racing career and went out of her way to help me gain a place in the World Championships Road Race. During the National Road Race Championships at Yeovil, Somerset, she kept coming back to help me to re-join the bunch when I lost touch with the main group after some of the steep hills on the route. In the end I persuaded her to carry on and she gained the Bronze medal that year and competed in the World Road Race Championship.

Sadly, Chris died from Cancer of the Spleen in the early 1980's at the age of 46 and it is a deep regret of mine that I didn't make a bigger effort to keep in touch with her. Often picking up a letter-card to write to her I found I was lost for words, not knowing

6

what to say. I learned a very hard lesson from the feeling that I had let her down and will never abandon a friend like that again.

I have lost touch with Janet Crowther but keep in touch with June Pitchford who I see occasionally.

From 1971 to 1974 I competed in the National 3000 metres Ladies Pursuit Championship and consistently won the bronze medal each year. Becoming frustrated by not making any progress, I contacted Alan Geldard (Bronze medalist in 1948 Olympic Games in men's 4000 metres team pursuit). He gave me guidance and coaching during 1975 and at that year's National 3000 metres Pursuit, I was in the final with Denise Burton (Beryl Burton's daughter). We were neck and neck – I'd be in the lead one lap, Denise on the next lap and the crowd were going crazy cheering us both on. I won the silver medal, losing the gold medal by 0.4 seconds. An improvement but soooo close to winning the title.

In 1974 I began a relationship with Andy Thompson who I later married in 1976. Andy rode in road races and in one racing season went from being a 3rd category racer to first category with several wins to his name. In football team terms, think local league to 1st Division. We would go out riding and training together and he would take great delight in sprinting away from me, forcing me to chase and then sprint away from me again. So exasperating but having the desired effect of pushing me to my limits.

In 1975, After Andy returned from a summer season racing in France, he started working with Dave Moulton (not Alex Moulton who created the Moulton bikes), making custom-built bicycle frames at Deblins Green, near Malvern. One of the first frames he built was a track frame for me and I'll never forget the first time I rode it on the track. My first words were 'I can breathe!'. Ever since I had been racing, particularly in the pursuit on the track, my breathing had been a problem and I could be heard all around the track. My position on the bike was hunched, compressing my lungs and ribs. Andy created a frame that released me so I could open up my lungs! My track frame measured 20.5 inches (52.07 cms) with a seat angle of 77 degrees and a head angle of 74 degrees – this enabled me to have a shorter than normal top tube. He later transferred the dimensions to a road racing frame that measured 20.75 inches (52.70 cms) with a 76 degree seat angle and 73 degree head tube angle.

When Andy Thompson and I married in 1976, we lived in Malvern, Worcestershire and again I needed to change cycling clubs. Here I joined then Gannet Cycling Club – based between Worcester and Hereford. Andy and I ran weekly training rides for our club during the winter months, often riding 80-miles on a Sunday. We also ran a couple of training weekends away to Builth Wells, Wales.

It was whilst Andy and I were members of the Gannet that I did my most prolific racing on the road and track, training with my club-mates and getting myself in the 'Scratch' group during our weekly 25-mile handicap training. 'Scratch' meant that I was in the fast group chasing all the other riders that has been set off ahead of us to give them an advantage.

One year, during the winter months, I joined a weight training club. I didn't lift heavy weights but weighing enough to give some resistance and I did lots of repetitions. I was flabbergasted at the results when I started racing later in the year. The upper body strength I had developed gave me a huge advantage over previous years and radically improved my climbing ability.

This in turn enabled me to do very effective interval training leading up to the National and World Championships where I developed a passable ability to sprint and gave me a 'killer' start at the beginning of a pursuit.

Andy supported me throughout my racing career and I know I couldn't have won my National titles in 1977 and 1978 without him. I shall expand on these two years racing later.

At the end of my cycle racing career, Gannet Cycling Club endowed me with Life Membership of the club for which I am very proud.

In 1979 Andy and I moved to Huddersfield and become members of the Holme Valley Wheelers. Here we set up The Thompson Bicycle Company Ltd, making custom-built bicycle frames. These were made-to-measure in the same way that someone would go to a Saville Row tailor for a suit. We soon became renowned locally, nationally and a few internationally for the quality of Andy's workmanship. My contribution was on the secretarial side along with filing the fillets of brazing and I became skilled at painting the lug-lines on the frames. We built frames for touring cyclists, club cyclists and many racing cyclists, most notable was Mandy Jones who won the Ladies National Pursuit Championship and the World Road Race Championship in 1982 on Thompson bikes. We also built a tandem for a time-trialling duo Dave Edlin and Graham Smith who broke Competition Record for 10-miles in 1980 with a time of 18.38. The most unusual order we had was to build two tandems for the Pleasance family, local to Huddersfield at the time. They sold their home so they could afford to ride around the world over three years with their children. On their return, their eldest son sailed through the 11-plus exam (still being held in Kent). Sadly, our business went into Receivership in 1982 following the Thatcher government's lack of support for small businesses and several costly mistakes we made. The effect was devastating to both of us feeling like a bereavement, made all the more difficult with twin boys Alex and Vincent just one year old.

In 1989 our marriage broke up and I feel the effects of losing our business accounted for a lot of the reasons, as we both had differing outlooks on how to deal with the trauma of it. I brought up the boys on my own with Andy having access to them too.

Now in my late 60's, I have been a member of Stourbridge Cycling Club for around 35 years. Occasionally, I take part in their 'flat' local club runs but am no longer able to keep up on their 'hilly' rides. I am also a member of Stourbug where I can have a choice of rides within my current ability. I also ride with a social group that meet and ride in North Worcestershire that is very convivial. Whilst I worked at Age UK Dudley from 2005 to 2014, I set up 'Get Cycling for 50 Plus' as a project to enable older people to enjoy the local canal towpaths, tracks and quiet lanes. At the time of writing, it is still an active group with a different name and operating under a different 'umbrella'

Chapter 3 – Track Racing

The first time I ever rode around a cycle track was at Halesowen Cycling and Athletic Club at Manor Abbey Stadium. I was still at school and it must have been 1968 or 1969. I should have been one of the competitors in the Midlands Schools Cross-Country Running event but had injured a tendon in my foot and couldn't run. Instead I went to cheer on my team-mates and took my bike. I had never seen a 'real' track before and couldn't resist having a ride around it. With no-one around to show me, I tried to ride on the track in a clockwise direction. No wonder it felt so strange, as I should have ridden in the normal anti-clockwise direction, but I didn't know any better at the time.

During 1971, whilst Roy and Kate Packwood were coaching me, they introduced me to track racing as they felt this type of racing would suit my ability. Once a week I was taken to Salford Park track, Erdington (Birmingham) where I competed mainly with schoolboys on a limited gear ratio of 82". On occasions I also competed in the handicap 1-lap sprint events where I was placed a long way in front of the senior male riders to give me a 'chance'. They soon sped past me and I felt like the 'hare' in greyhound races. The scariest races were called 'Devil-take-the-Hindmost' (now called the Elimination Race) where the bunch ride around the track and every lap the last person is pulled out of the race. The consequence of this is that the bunch 'concertinas' as the leading riders slow down once they have crossed the line and the back riders speed up to keep in the race. I never lasted more than 3 laps … it was too scary.

Having competed in many time trial events since joining the Evesham & District Wheelers in 1968 and recording decent times over 10 miles, I wanted to have a go at riding the 3000 metre pursuit, which is equivalent to 1.86 miles. My club mates and coach felt I had the ability to 'go for it'. The first time I rode at this distance was in May 1971 at Salford Track and I recorded 4 minutes 21 seconds.

Carol Barton from Long Eaton Paragon, who would become a notable adversary won with 4 minutes 15 seconds. For the first time, I realised I might have a talent at this distance and could hold my own against the fastest ladies. Over the coming years Carol would deny me the opportunity to move up the podium places many times.

1971 was the first year I competed in the National Pursuit Championships where I came across the formidable Beryl Burton from Morley CC, Leeds. Since the 1960's she had won five World titles at both road and track World Championships. None of the other British ladies could get close to her and she had become my 'idol' – I could barely believe I was competing at the same National Championship as her! The event took place at Kirkby Stadium, Liverpool and I was delighted to have raced through the preliminary heats, quarter finals and semi finals. Due to atrocious weather conditions, the finals had to take place a week later and, to my delight, I won the bronze medal in a time of 4 minutes 28 seconds. Beryl Burton won in a time of 4 minutes 16 seconds and Bernadette Swinnerton from Stoke C and AC took the silver in 4 minutes 22 seconds. Confirmation again that the time I produced was of national standard.

Also in 1971 I made an attempt to create a ladies record for 1-hour on Salford Track. The distance I covered was 22 miles, 260 yards (35.6 kms), which I was disappointed with at the time. In retrospect, it wasn't at all bad - I'm sure I could have bettered it in later years once I had more speed and experience. The World record as at September 2018 by Vittoria Bussi from Italy is 48 kms (29.8 miles) at a Mexico velodrome, wearing a skinsuit – I rode on an open track with just shorts and T-shirt, 47 years earlier.

Immediately before taking part in races, I used to get very nervous – as most competitors do. It's part of psyching a competitor up so that the Adrenalin flows to enable them to activate the 'fight or flight' response and help them perform at their best. If I didn't feel the 'butterflies' sufficiently before a race, my performance suffered. Having said that, I used to allow my stress levels to get out of control, resulting in practically no performance at all and that dampened my confidence.

I remember the worst 'attack' I experienced of this was just as I arrived at Leicester track for the Ladies National Pursuit Championship, possibly 1973 or 1974. I looked around the car park and I could see Beryl Burton's car so I knew she would win. Perhaps I could gain silver if my other adversaries didn't attend. To my utter dismay, Carol Barton arrived, and I broke down in floods of tears, knowing (having convinced myself) I would only gain the bronze medal …. again.

I look back on this time feeling sad that I didn't have sufficient 'self-belief' and my mindset was beaten before I had turned a pedal. This was before Andy Thompson became a part of my life and with his help and ability to help me to relax during the late 1970's, he guided and pushed me into achieving results I wouldn't have dreamed of on my own.

Since 2009 a new passion has come into my life in the form of Laughter Yoga, which is a great stress reliever, boosts the immune system, increases the net supply of oxygen into the body and brain and is thoroughly uplifting. Laughter Yoga is a combination of role-playing everyday activities with laughter, hand claps and deep breathing and is very uplifting too. How I wish I had been aware of it during my cycle racing days.

Chapter 4 – Lands End to John O'Groats (Stage 1)

Why did I want to ride Lands End to John O'Groats (LEJOG)?

I had often heard about people cycling Lands End to John O'Groats and dreamed about doing it one day – when I could find enough time to devote to it. Life in general and responsibilities got in the way of realising it for many years.

Steve, my partner, cycled John O'Groats to Lands End in 1997 and often told me tales of his adventures over five weeks whilst he included lots of extra excursions to the furthest East and the furthest West along his route and also riding through Wales.

With retirement age creeping up on me and wanting to be certain I would still have the ability to complete this epic tour, I began to plan how I would achieve it. Still working full time and wanting to have a 'normal' holiday with Steve as well, the only way I could make it a reality was to split it into three sections, riding one week at a time over three separate years.

This is the first part of story of my adventure starting in April 2010, which I deliberately completed on my own in order to have a unique experience.

Map of my complete route

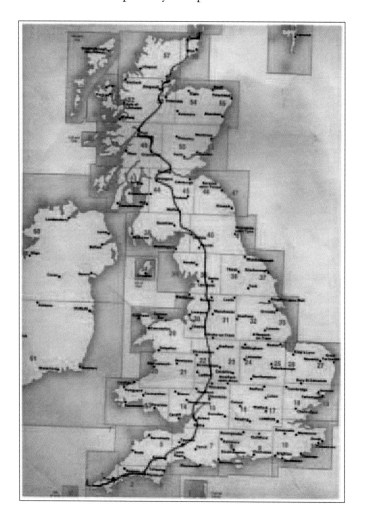

Prologue   Distance11 miles

Well, that was an eventful start …..

The logistics of cycling Lands End to John O'Groats meant that I needed to use the train to reach my start point at Lands End. I left Stourbridge Junction with my fully loaded bike and when I reached New Street Station in Birmingham there had been a power cut and the emergency back-up also failed. Everyone was evacuated from the station whilst they made repairs and my train to Exeter St Davids left 45-minutes late.

Arriving at Exeter, the delay in Birmingham meant that I'd missed my connection and had to take the slower, but more scenic route to Penzance to complete my journey. As we approached Penzance, St Michael's Mount appeared out of the mist – one of those 'Wow!' moments.

Working full time when I took on this challenge at the age of 58 led me to decide to split it into 3 stages, taking a week off work to do each stage over a period of 3 years. At the time I started this challenge, I knew the record for a woman cycling this distance was 2 days, 4 hours, 45 minutes and 11 seconds by LEA Taylor in 2002 but I didn't want to race through the scenery, I wanted to take in all its delights, highs and lows so that I could take in the whole experience.

Being a member of CTC (Cyclists Touring Club), now called 'Cycling UK' I'd downloaded the "LEJOG' route plan from their website and used it as my guide for the whole journey, making detours on various sections that I particularly wanted to visit.

So, here I was at Penzance in late afternoon with my loaded Trek Hybrid with a round trip of 25 miles to ride to Lands End and back to officially 'start' my adventure. Isn't it strange how, after a long rail journey, the body still feels as though it is 'moving' with the 'ghost' sensation of 'da da da – daaah' as if still on the rail tracks.

Soon I found NCN3 (National Cycle Network) and followed

it all the way to Lands End – what a delight! I rode through pretty Mousehole after which I headed inland and passed quite a lot of menhirs including the Merry Maidens small stone circle, which dates back to late Neolithic. I could feel myself relax and enjoy the ride as I continued to St Buryan.

I passed the 'Last Pub in England' and as I reached the final half-mile I felt the first few spots of rain and high winds. I was sorry to see the 'Theme Park' at the end of the road – the last time I'd been to Lands End in 1980 it had been a simple, pretty and genuine landmark. Visibility was now about 100 yards so I could just about see the rocky seascape but its beauty was lost today although it did have an air of mystery. Unfortunately, the Theme Park was closed as I'd arrived too late to have my 'official' photograph taken, so I found a place to take a photo of my bike against a wall with a rocky sea-scape behind it to 'prove' I had been there. I then headed back to Penzance, passing the 'First Pub in England'. It went completely out of my mind to call in to ask them to put their stamp on my record sheet to prove I'd been at Lands End!

Finally, I arrived at the beautifully renovated Penzance Youth Hostel, which would be my home for the night. I chatted to a young man from Essex who was taking the summer off to walk various sections of England's coastal paths and travelling between by bus.

2 Penzance to Fowey   Distance 64 miles

Cornwall and Devon are renowned as being the hilliest sections of the Lands End to John O'Groats route. Perhaps it just seems that way as it is the beginning of this epic challenge and the legs have not yet 'warmed-up' to the task in hand. I found that there was very little flat and that the terrain was either up or down short, but very sharp, hills. The recompense was that it was absolutely stunning.

A damp start but not raining and a belly full of a hearty breakfast, I set off into Penzance and cycled to Marazion with the view to my right of a mist shrouded St Michael's Mount. I was delighted the tide was out so I could walk the causeway to the mount – this was wide enough to take vehicles and was made of large stone cobblestones. I left my bike at Marazion and felt rather awkward, trying to walk the causeway wearing cycling shoes with the cleats on the bottom making me slide on the stones.

Evidence of man living on St Michael's Mount goes back to the Bronze Age and the church at the top was built following the Norman Conquest with links to the Benedictine Abbey at Mont St Michel in France. The castle is still home to the St Aubyn family as it has been since medieval times.

Riding out of Marazion, I rode inland up Godolphin Hill where I saw the first of many tin mine engine house ruins. Relics of a by-gone age, these ivy-clad towering chimneys set the imagination racing, conjuring up what life must have been like when they were at their height. I almost hoped to see Ross Poldark appear around a corner!

At Porkellis I missed my turning and after a mile or so couldn't understand why the wind was against me instead of helping, so I retraced right back to the entrance to the village and found my road by a pub at the top of a hill.

Already quite a hilly ride, I was glad to make contact with a couple of friends who have moved to Cornwall and invited me to have lunch with them. The wonders of mobile phones – Bruce met me at a junction of a small village and directed me to the farm he and Nina were renting at the time. They gave me a huge, delicious meal. It was great to catch up and reminisce, as I hadn't seen them for several years

Setting off again I rode to Perranwell and on to Tressilick to take the King Harry Ferry, which made a very loud clunking noise as the chain that drove the ferry rubbed against something metallic.

I would have liked to take a more scenic route but needed to catch up some time and distance, so I went along the main 'A' road to Tregony and found some relief from constant climbing. Then I took the 'B' road to Hawes Water with a good tailwind at my back.

Many parts of Cornwall have unusual dry-stone walls in a herring-bone pattern called 'Curzeyway' and I was charmed to see some examples along my route. Soon, I could see white, conical hills in the distance and wondered what they were – they turned out to be the china clay heaps behind St Austell. What a sprawling place St Austell is. Thankfully I was able to bypass it to Carlyon Bay and joined the 'A' road heading for Fowey.

It was getting late and when I checked my map I realised I'd omitted to include the crucial section leading me along tiny lanes to reach Golant Youth Hostel just outside Fowey. I stopped to telephone the hostel to let them know I was nearly there and asked for directions. I also asked them to keep an evening meal for me as there were no pubs nearby to the hostel and this had been a long, hard ride. I finally arrived at this lovely Georgian mansion at 7.50 pm having ridden 64 miles. I hungrily ate a huge vegetable pizza for supper.

3 Fowey to Plymouth   Distance 37 miles

Refreshed after a good sleep, the girls at Golant Youth Hostel kitchen did me proud with a delicious breakfast of mushrooms on toast. I chatted to a couple on holiday from Nottinghamshire and they kindly sponsored me as I am raising funds through this ride for Get Cycling for 50 Plus – a project with Age UK Dudley with whom I worked at the time, which I set up as part of my role as LEAP Over 50 Project co-ordinator (LEAP is an acronym for Leisure, Exercise and Activity for people – over 50).

Setting off, I took it very gently back up the long hill to the main road. It was only 1¼ miles and seemed shorter than it did last night.

As I rode into Fowey I was totally enchanted by the most unusual bus stop I've ever seen – set up like a summer-house at the side of the road by someone who obviously loves Vincent Van Gogh's Sunflowers.

I headed along a very narrow road to reach the ferry to Bodinick. Riding up-hill the other side was very slow business and I finally reached the top at Lanteglos Highway. Deciding not to stay on the main road I turned off right towards Peakswater and immediately recognised it as I place I'd stayed at years ago in a static caravan. It was delightful to cycle along the narrow lane where the road verges were a mass of Celandines and trees coming into leaf. I continued along this pretty lane to Pelynt where I joined the main 'A' road (A3359) through 'Barcelona' (no signs to photograph!) and on down a long hill to West Looe.

Wandering along the narrow streets through the shops and the beach, I decided to find somewhere for lunch and saw a sign for Daisy's Café up a little side street. What a little gem – and I was made to feel most welcome. The young lady explained that the soup of the day was Sweet Potato and Coconut milk – how could I resist! It was delicious – served with huge cheese scones and apple juice. I enjoyed it so much I asked for the recipe and have made it many times at home since.

Fortified, I set off again up a long hill to St Martin where the church and graveyard was festooned with wild primroses. After a couple of miles I went down a tremendous descent to Hessonford where I screeched to a halt. (My odometer recorded the speed of 36.8 mph on the descent!) I turned right and opted for a route via Seaton and Downderry as the map looked more scenic and right by the sea. Good decision – it was far quieter and the road down to Seaton was a gentle tree-lined descent with the scent of wild garlic filling my nostrils – who could ask for more! Seaton was shrouded in sea mist (making it feel very eerie) with a short, sharp climb at the other end to Downderry. This was a long village hugging the cliffs to the sea, none of which I could see due to the sea mist.

Out of Downderry was a long climb alongside a little stream. The road was undulating to Crafthole where I was very much aware I must be missing some spectacular sea views as I watched the mist billow eerily across the road from the sea. At Crafthole there was an unusual pub called the Finnygook Inn (15th century) and the sign depicted a skeleton ghoul holding a lantern – there's a smugglers tale to tell here. The inn was named after a notorious smuggler called Silas Finny who 'grassed' on his fellow smugglers following a disagreement and was murdered nearby.

As I turned inland towards Anthony I looked back and the sea mist appeared to be creeping after me – spooky. Taking a quieter road to the right I rode past HMS Raleigh to avoid the main traffic into Torcross where I took the ferry to Plymouth. To my astonishment there was no charge for bicycles (after £1.50 for Bodinnick and 50p for Tressilick). I chatted to another cyclist on board – a rugby player recovering from a knee replacement, getting fit again using his bike.

A big naval destroyer crossed the path of the ferry so we had to wait for it. I could just make out the Tamar Bridge in the distance; strange to think that only 2 days ago I'd crossed the Tamar on the rail bridge on my way down to Penzance by train.

I headed for Plymouth Hoe and was pleased to see Smeaton's Tower but it too had mist swirling around it. This was an Eddystone lighthouse designed by John Smeaton and was in use until 1877, after which it was moved to the Hoe. I also saw the statue of Sir Francis Drake commemorating his circumnavigation of the globe. He'd actually 'taken' California for Queen Elizabeth the First, calling it Nova Albion and the statue was a gift from California in the 1970's.

I reached my B&B at the Tudor Hotel around 5.00 pm having

ridden 37 miles. After settling in I went for a walk and to find somewhere to eat – the mist had cleared and I could see Islands across Plymouth Sound but the mist still hugged land on Coxside. I had a better view of Smeaton's Tower and passed by the Royal Citadel. The Citadel was built in the late 1660's on the site of an earlier fort. As I turned left towards the Barbican, Mount Batten's peninsular was in front of me. I carried on down to the harbour by the lock gate where there was a tremendous sculpture of a sea monster on a tall pedestal – I have since discovered this is the Plymouth Prawn and was erected in 1996.

I continued to walk towards the Elizabethan House and came across the Village Restaurant where I took a table for one. I'd just ordered when another lady came in also asking for a table for one so I invited her to join me. Jenny and I spent the rest of the evening chatting like long lost friends and both knew our life histories by the end of the evening.

4 Plymouth to Exeter   Distance 50 miles

I overslept! Must have been last night's wine! Got up quickly and had breakfast.

As I mentioned in previously, I worked for Age UK Dudley when I was doing this ride and had taken a week's holiday in order to complete the first stage of Lands End to John O'Groats'. I asked people I met to give me donations for my ride so my scheme could raise funds to cover some expenses of running the Get Cycling for 50 Plus project. On my route, I had arranged to call at various other Age UK charity offices and today I arrived at Age UK Plymouth for a meeting and photo-shoot by 9.40 am and they were most welcoming. Several of them sponsored me and a member of staff helped me locate the Plym Valley Cycle Route.

His instructions were perfect, I was so glad to get away from the noisy traffic. The cycle route reminded me of a similar one near where I live but this has a tarmac surface and a slight incline to Clearbrook. Just before the end - 6 miles away - I arrived at 'the tunnel' and stood before it for a few moments psyching myself up to ride through it as tunnels spook me. I could see there were small lights about 60 cm from the floor spaced every 180 cm or so and gingerly started riding in, having turned on my front light. Soon the tunnel turned a corner to the left and the light shone back in from the other side – I was so relieved as I was through in less than 100 metres!

I left the route a short distance from the tunnel as it disintegrated and the lane looked more inviting. No sooner had I done so there was a very steep hill – possibly 1:6, which I walked up. I joined the main road to Yelverton and then took the 'B' road (B3212), which I stayed on all the way to Exeter. One of the steepest sections was on the way out of Yelverton onto Dartmoor. I took several photos en-route to Pricetown, utterly taken aback by its wild beauty and remoteness.

I had fantastic weather conditions for this ride – a tailwind, bright and sunny with good visibility – there can't be many 'perfect' days to cross Dartmoor like today. I was glad to find the hills were quite manageable in my lowest gear and the descents were fabulous.

From Princetown I rode on to Two Bridges where I stopped for my picnic and was struck by the contrast where the moor had been 'tamed' with pockets of civilisation. I chatted to a couple at the pub and then set off towards Postbridge. The vastness of the moors was overwhelming and I stopped several times to take photos.

Soon I could see views beyond Dartmoor towards Moretonhampstead and stopped to take a picture of Dartmoor Ponies just before a tremendous descent. Then the climbing really began – 3 miles to Duccombe – it was the hardest climb of the day. I turned a corner near Dunsford and I saw about 12 Alpacas – they had such cute faces and were as inquisitive of me as I was of them.

My legs felt pretty tired on the final approach to Exeter – one hill after another. I reached a huge roundabout by the River Exe and asked a lady whether there was a cycle route to Countess Wear where the Youth Hostel was located. She was most helpful and 4 miles later after a delightful riverside ride I arrived at the Youth Hostel. I had a quick shower and supper of leek and potato soup, spaghetti Bolognese, and ice cream. There was a party of French youngsters on a school trip too and I enjoyed 'ear-wigging' the youngsters and understanding a lot of what they were saying.

5 Exeter to Glastonbury   Distance 65 miles

I chatted with a Scandinavian lady from my dormitory during breakfast – she had also been at Penzance Youth Hostel at the same time I was there. She came from Sweden and works as a milk-maid at the moment, milking 50 cows at a farm. Having been in England touring for 4 weeks, she's returning home shortly having also visited Spain, Australia, New Zealand and Iceland and particularly recommended riding horses in Iceland.

I rode back along the river path to Age UK Exeter, another charity office I had arranged to call at where I met some members of staff. They made me very welcome and we chatted about their projects and mine and took photos. Before leaving Exeter, I went to see the cathedral and asked the driver at Exeter Bus Station for directions to Honiton – I struck gold as his directions were perfect.

The lane I took to Honiton was very busy and I hoped it would quieten down after Exeter airport. It didn't - despite it running parallel to the even busier A30. There was quite a cross-wind and long drags of hills so I was glad to reach Honiton, but it was a real disappointment. I didn't see much worth speaking of other than an

24

information sign about the 'Trafalgar Way'.

Apparently, Honiton was the 8th horse change out of 21 made by Lieutenant John Richard Lapenotiere between Falmouth and London in November 1805, when he rode for 37 hours to cover 271 miles. He brought the news to the Prime Minister and the King about victory at Trafalgar and the death of Lord Nelson.

After Honiton I found some pleasant lanes at last but I found myself climbing some monumental hills - several I had to walk up. I really haven't mastered the art of walking up hills with my bike whilst wearing cycling shoes with cleats on the bottom – I must look like a demented Max Wall from behind! My legs kept being 'bumped' by my panniers and the cleats on my shoes slipped on the tarmac and I generally kept falling over myself!

I climbed to the village of Cotleigh and sat in the churchyard eating my lunch. Then I dropped down a fantastic descent only to have to climb again to the top of Stockland Hill. I now had a favourable tailwind but reckoned it was going to take me an hour to do the 6 miles to Chard. It was a real roller-coaster and, as I reached the plateau, I crossed into Somerset and joined an 'A' road for a short distance into Chard.

This was a nice town where I treated myself to 2 cakes! Heading slightly north I took the 'A' road (A358), I was pleased to find I was making much better progress with a good tailwind. The sun came out (it had been cool and dull before) as I rode through the charming town of Ilminster. My next town was Shepton Beauchamp. It was now pretty well flat and I was on the Somerset levels here and, with a tailwind, I was regularly riding at 14 mph.

What a delight Somerton is with many old buildings in local stone (looks very like Cotswold). There was a row of Almshouses, a Butter Cross and other lovely honey-coloured buildings. I was also delighted to see that Glastonbury was only 8 miles away and it was only 6.00 pm. The ride was going well until I had to climb Collard Hill to Marshall Elm – I really didn't want another big climb after riding 60 miles. However, my reward at the top was a magical view of Glastonbury Tor.

I descended into Street but was rather disappointed in the place, which had quite a run-down feel about it. A couple more miles and I reached Glastonbury and arrived at Karuna House B&B at 7.30 pm. My host was warm and welcoming and showed me my room saying I could use her meditation studio if I wished. There were lots of nice shops and café's but very few were open for evening meals at 8.30 pm. In the end I opted for an Indian meal. Afterwards, I went back to Karuna House and chatted with my delightful host.

6 Glastonbury to Bristol   Distance 35 miles

I woke up to the sound of birdsong. After a hearty breakfast, I loaded the bike but left it outside Karuna House whilst I had a walk around Glastonbury.

I headed for the Abbey and joined a party of French students from Britanny. One of their teachers was pretty knowledgeable so I tagged along listening to his lecture. The abbey was very rich – second only to Westminster at the time of the dissolution in 1539 (assets of £4,000). Joseph of Arimathea founded the monastery in the 8th century and it later became a Benedictine order. It was reputed that King Arthur and Guinevere are buried here so it became a place of pilgrimage. I followed the group into the abbot's kitchen where a 'monk' explained life at the height of its time. They ate fish and 1kg of bread a day. They also ate beavers – 'as it swam like a fish'. During the summer they ate swallows as they appeared in May and disappeared in September – it was thought they too came from the river!

It had begun to rain quite heavily, which was a bit disappointing but at least I only had to ride to Bristol today. I collected the bike and was grateful my host had put a bin liner over my saddle. I then undid all her good work as, when I put my bags in the top bag over my back wheel, a water puddle on it ran down onto my saddle, soaking my back-side! The first 6 miles were pretty straight forward to Wells. I stopped here to look at the magnificent cathedral and wished I'd taken the opportunity to go inside but was concerned to leave my laden bike outside, as there were a lot of people around. The cathedral square was magnificent - I thought 'Eat your heart out Sacre Coeur!' As I was about to leave I heard someone say 'Maggie?' I turned around to see four people who turned out to be members of a walking group from my workplace! They were on holiday and had attended the previous Saturday afternoon's walk, so were aware I was doing this bike ride. What a coincidence! I was sorry not to have taken a photo of them – I was too flabbergasted to think of such things.

Next, I set off towards Wookey Hole and more climbing, which wasn't too bad even though the weather was very soggy. I recognised where the caves were and the paper mill having visited them about 20 years ago. I then started a very long climb and eventually made it to the top, but half way up I encountered the only arrogant motorist so far who barely gave me enough room whilst he was coming down!

I rode on to the Queen Victoria pub at Priddy where a cycling club from Bristol were sat by a nice open fire. I was pretty wet and soggy from the persistent rain so put my coat over the chair to protect it. The rowdy cyclists soon went and I enjoyed a delicious hot chocolate whilst chatting to local farmers and making a fuss of a 'bear' of a 3 year old white, long haired Alsatian dog – he was magnificent.

I rode on through Chew Stoke and Winford, which weren't shown at their best in the damp weather conditions. I manage to miss a turning up a very steep hill but climbed Long Ashton hill. I was so glad to turn off the main road – it was scary with very heavy traffic as it was now around 5.00 pm.

Soon I saw a signpost showing Clifton was 3 miles away – nearly there! Luckily there was a road directly to the suspension bridge that was only open to residents, walkers and cyclists. There were some rather exclusive houses along this lane and I took a photo through some trees looking down the Avon Gorge. As I reached the bridge a grumpy official demanded I get off the footpath and ride on the road, which was narrow and heavy with traffic.

Once on the other side, I immediately walked the bike back along the footpath to take a photo from the bridge – there was a sign with a number to contact for the Samaritans should anyone be so depressed they would contemplate taking their life from this bridge. From here I had a game trying to find my way to the Youth Hostel and asked people several times for directions to the docks. It was a long descent and I eventually found it on the quay; the building had originally been a corn store.

The girl on reception was very helpful and I was able to put my bike in the basement. I walked across the bridge to the 'Pitcher & Piano'. It was very much a 20 and 30 year olds hang out and very noisy due to the 'acoustics' of this old warehouse building but the food was good. Back at the hostel, I sat in the lounge with another cyclist from Reading who was planning to ride back along the Kennett and Avon canal with his friend the next day.

7 Bristol to Ledbury   Distance 66 miles

As the Youth Hostel had previously been a grain store, I had a fitful night's sleep as it was noisy. I fetched my bike from the store, loaded up and went in search of Age UK Bristol located about a mile away. Here I met the staff and spent an interesting half an hour discussing similar projects and had a photo shoot outside their office.

Then I set off to find the SS Great Britain – I had wanted to see this ship for many years, having passed signs for in on the M5 during many journeys to visit my father who lived in Torquay at the end of his life. I am fascinated by history and the Industrial Revolution in this instance. Living in the West Midlands, I am surrounded by evidence of the transformations this era brought to the UK and the world. SS Great Britain was the first iron ship ever built 160 years ago by Isambard Kingdom Brunel. It paved the way for modern ship design as we know it. Firstly, I looked at the hull in dry dock and even the propeller was a revolutionary design – the ship was expected to be a paddle steamer but Brunel designed the propeller and rudder instead. I visited the museum that described parts of construction and major sailings and how it was grounded for years in the Falkland Islands before being rescued in the 1970's and brought back to Bristol. I was able to go on deck where livestock would have been housed - to be eaten during long voyages. I went below decks to the tiny cabins and bunks for the sailors. The next deck down there was a most opulent dining room – for 1st class passengers I presume.

It was 11.00 am when I left the SS Great Britain. I had been so engrossed in my visit I completely forgot time. I chided myself for being so crazy when I had 60-miles to ride – I would now be under pressure to reach Ledbury in daylight! I set off uphill through the city to Clifton Downs where there were some very classy houses. I then headed for Westbury on Trym and was soon in the countryside with familiar farm smells in the air. However, who said it would be a flat ride to the Severn Bridge?

I continued to Almondsbury where I stopped on a bench for lunch, watching a glowering sky threatening heavy rain heading my way. As the first raindrops fell, I put on wet weather gear including overshoes and set off again, watching the sky as much as the road and bracing myself for a very wet ride.

I continued through Olveston and then to the Severn Bridge itself. There was a special track beside the road (a virtual motorway) that was open to walkers and cyclists. The bridge is over 2 miles long and as I rode onto it, I could feel the vibrations from the heavy traffic (particularly if I got off the bike). I was able to look upstream and took a couple of photos – including the sheets of rain falling over the Forest of Dean where I was heading. I felt the effects of quite a strong side wind and was grateful the path was slightly lower than the road carrying the traffic and the strong railings on the other side keeping me safe.

About half way across the storm hit me – literally! It was as though buckets of water were being thrown at me and I was drenched within seconds. By the time I reached the end of the bridge, the storm had abated but it was still raining and I was dripping wet.

I carried on to a large roundabout and was able to continue into Chepstow and very briefly into Wales along the NCN4 (National Cycle Network) cycle route. What a delightful town. I had a superb descent through it, passing an old gateway down to the bridge over the River Wye just before its confluence with the River Severn. I was now back in England and climbed through Tutshill, hugging the River Wye into the Forest of Dean.

Would you believe it – the sun came out again and I saw no more rain for the rest of the day. I rode through Woodcroft and then typical Forest of Dean woodland that was undulating rather than major hills to St Briavels. I made a detour here to go to the castle, which was a Youth Hostel – I hoped it might have a café but was out of luck as it was already 4.00 pm. It was only another 4½ miles to Coleford so I made the most of the tailwind and rode hard to get there before the café's shut. I found one – not particularly inspiring but enjoyed a hot chocolate and cake. Riding on to Broadwell I had one of the most spectacular descents of the whole trip down to Cannop (38.4 mph!). At the cross roads I turned left along to Lydbrook, mainly following contour lines. Glancing into the forest I briefly saw a deer – it saw me and vanished. Another tremendous descent to Stowfield where there is a major road junction with the River Wye immediately ahead. I turned right towards Ross on Wye and as I rode with the river to my left, there was a huge field of

Oilseed in full flower – it looked stunning and its pungent scent was almost overpowering. Soon I reached Ross on Wye where I rode about ½ mile to the M50 roundabout and turned off onto an 'A' road (A449) – nearly on home territory.

Being so close it seemed to take forever to reach Much Marcle where I stopped to phone Steve, my partner (it was now after 7.00 pm). I continued past the Sling Inn and on to Rushall – I had about 7 more miles to go. As I rode through Kynaston, it was comforting to see Ledbury in the distance with a foreground of another field of Oilseed so took my last photos of the day. Soon I was in Little Marcle Lane and arrived at Steve's at 7.55 pm.

It was wonderful to be with Steve and to tell him about my adventures over a mug of tea and cake. Once I was cleaned up we enjoyed a pleasant meal and evening together. We chatted the rest of the evening, catching up on news. I phoned my Mum too, so she knew I'd reached Steve's.

8 Ledbury to Stourbridge   Distance 47 miles

The wind direction changed today to north east so would be against me to Stourbridge. After a couple of days relaxing with Steve he joined me as far as Knightwick. We rode out of Ledbury to Staplow under a sky full of threatening clouds and sunshine on a day significantly colder than any last week. Our ride took us through Bosbury to Westfield to the west of Cradley. Being weighed down by 2 panniers Steve was up ahead of me on his light road bike. We rode on to Grittlesend where there is a very steep but short hill and continued to Suckley, stopping in the porch of Suckley Church for our picnic. We stopped briefly at the White House at Suckley Green to look at the ornate porch just before the first heavy downpour enveloped us as we headed for Knightwick. Diving into The Talbot

Inn, we had delicious hot chocolate, getting warmed and dried out a bit before parting our separate ways.

I now had one of the steepest climbs of the tour – Ankerdine Hill that is 1:4 in places. I took this very gently as I was practically riding it from a 'cold' start. Reaching the top I was rewarded by one of the best views of the Malvern Hills I've seen from this vantage point.

I continued to Martley then on to Wichenford. Just before reaching the village I took the turn for Ockeridge. I was now beginning to see signs to places I was very familiar with as they are within a day's ride from my home and it felt very comforting. I turned right to Holt Heath and after crossing the bridge over the River Severn at Holt Fleet I rode along one of my favourite lanes to Lineholt and Lincomb. Pretty as ever in this springtime, I savoured this route of many clubruns all the way to Hartlebury. I rode under the 'A' road (A449) and over the level crossing towards Elmley Lovett.

At this level crossing a few years ago I had spectacularly nearly lost my bike on a clubrun when I leant it against the gates as a train was coming through. The gates started to raise when all was clear and I became aware that my bike was still attached – I removed it at lightning speed otherwise it would have hung helplessly until the next time a train was due and the gates were lowered again! It caused much hilarity amongst my cycling friends.

Another heavy rain shower around Elmley Lovett and soon I was heading down familiar lanes to Chaddesley Corbett where I took my last photograph of this stage as it is a pretty village. I chose to ride via Hillpool and then through Hackmans Gate to Hagley and into Stourbridge. At Oldswinford the heaviest rain shower of the day hit me as I rode round the ring road and on to my Mum's home at Wordsley. Stripping off my soggy cycling clothes, it was lovely to see her and tell her all about my adventure, showing her my photographs too. She was relieved I was back and seemed fairly well.

After spending an hour or so with her I put on my wet cycling clothes and rode the last 1½ miles home where I was greeted by a very excited Tinker, my cat.   Having finished the first leg of the LEJOG ride, I now cannot wait until I'm on the road again next year when I shall ride from Stourbridge to Glasgow.

Photos from Stage 1:

Maggie's loaded bike at Lands End

St Michael's Mount, near Penzance

Bus Stop fit for a Queen – Fowey

Plymouth Prawn at The Barbican

Cycling over Dartmoor in perfect conditions towards
Moretonhampstead

Glastonbury Tor from Collard Hill at Marsh Elm

Oilseed in bloom, River Wye and Lydbrook

Malvern Hills from Collins Green – above Ankerdine Hill

37

Chapter 5 – 1977 National Pursuit Championships

Following my marriage to Andy Thompson in 1976, we both returned to our cycle racing, joining the Gannet Cycling Club and enjoying being able to train together around the Malvern Hills, Herefordshire and the Severn Valley.

We ran training rides on Sunday mornings during the winter months, covering around 80 miles each ride to build up our endurance. One evening each week during this time, we used to ride in a club group around the West Malvern Road to the Wych Cutting, along Jubilee Drive to British Camp and then descend to Little Malvern, Malvern Wells and back to Great Malvern. It was only a 9-mile circuit but severely hilly, particularly the West Malvern Road.

Later in the year we would have group training along a 25-mile circuit, which would be split into groups according to each person's ability. My club mate Shirley Davis and I went off first and were gradually caught by the faster groups behind us. We used to try to extend how long it took the others to catch us each time. In my final year, I joined the fast group, catching the slower riders. We used to have club time trials too, generally around 10-miles distance.

During the winters of 1976-78, I tried weight training as I heard it was very beneficial for building muscle and strength. The weights I used were not particularly heavy but I concentrated on frequent repetitions. I was astounded by the effect when I rode my first races the following season! I was strong enough to climb the hills better than I had ever done before! The men had included weight training during the winter for many years but only a small handful of women were using it at that time. It was a game-changer for me and helped to build my confidence.

Having come second to Denise Burton in the Ladies National Pursuit by a two-fifths of a second in 1975, my training and racing was geared to improving my speed and endurance for 3000 metres for 1977. My level of confidence had grown enormously. Gone were the days when I actually burst out crying at the sight of one of my major competitors, resigning myself through my thoughts to losing. My intensive interval training in the lead up to the National Pursuit at the beginning of August were paying off, along with the confidence building talks Andy gave me during our training sessions and at home.

Interval training consisted of a 5-mile gentle ride to a flat circuit to the east of Malvern at Gualford that was 1-mile around. At 3 points around the circuit I would sprint 'flat out' for around 100 metres or so and then just allow the bike to coast slowly to the next point, at which I would repeat the sprint. I would ride around the circuit 5 times doing 3 sprints each time – 15 sprints in all. I would then 'crawl' the 5 miles back home, totally shattered. This helped me to develop a 'killer' start when racing a pursuit.

The day of the Ladies National Pursuit arrived and I did a good time in the preliminary heats, catching my opponent in the quarter-final. As my time was the fastest, I was drawn the slowest rider in the semi-final. This meant I drew Cathy Swinnerton whilst Denise and Beryl Burton rode against each other – this was an extraordinary situation for them both – mother and daughter in the same semi-final. I beat Catherine and then Denise beat Beryl.

The finals were held off until the next day due to weather conditions and it was with great trepidation that I waited for my turn to compete in the final for the gold or silver medal. Those few minutes whilst the bronze medal heat was taking place were like torture in the anticipation of my final result. My stomach churned, thoughts were all over the place. Could I get a fast enough start? Would Denise have her customary killer fast finish? Would my energy die before I reached the finish line?

Then it was my turn to race for gold or silver against Denise … I was at the starting gate, the time keeper gave me 30 seconds … 10 seconds … then beep, beep, beep, beep, beep … beeeep!

I was off and had a good strong start. The interval training I had been doing ensured I had a very fast start, almost being able to see Denise in the same straight. I had to sustain this speed and the middle laps are always the most difficult as the body begins to tire from the effort. Aware of Denise's fast finish, I had to pull more speed out of the bag in the closing laps.

AT LAST ….. I DID IT! I became Ladies National Pursuit Champion. My time for 3000 metres was 4.10.29 and Denise finished with 4.13.88. I was ecstatic! Beryl took the bronze medal beating Cathy Swinnerton.

That wasn't the end of the story. In 1976 Denise Burton beat Beryl Burton in the Ladies National Road Race and a split in the family that had been brewing for months finally blew up. Beryl refused to shake hands with her daughter on the victory podium. From what I understand, Denise had not been pulling her weight around the family home. She had been following the more modern approach to cycle racing that encouraged plenty of rest in between racing and training. Beryl on the other hand ran the home, worked full time at a rhubarb farm and rode her bike everywhere as her training.

In later years, having had twin boys myself and been run ragged working full time only to find washing up piled high waiting to be done and half eaten yoghurt pots hidden under their beds, I can relate to Beryl's simmering anger. On the other hand, I can understand Denise wanting to train and ride her race her own way using modern techniques. After all, I embraced the use of weight training during the winter months that had a transformational effect on my strength in early season races. However, it was very sad that she couldn't share her daughter's winning moment, such was Beryl's sheer will to win.

When it became clear that neither Beryl nor Denise had the form to beat me in the National Pursuit, it was one of the catalysts that helped to bring the family back together and they shared hugs in the track centre during the event. The fact that I had a small part to play in their reconciliation touches my heart deeply and, in the long term, has left me feeling more uplifted than any title I could have won.

A touching moment on the podium was when we were all being presented with our medals and I felt a bit awkward, never having been in that position before. Beryl quietly whispered to me to wave my hands to the cheering crowd – that was so gracious of her.

Chapter 6 – Road Racing 1978

7 to 9-7-78 Course Cycliste Feminine International

Great Britain sent a team of 4 ladies to compete in this 3-day stage race in the area of Le Havre, Seine-Maritime, France. The team comprised Cathy Swinnerton, Terrie Riley, Hilda Barrie and myself.

The prologue event was a 1200 metre time trial, which would have been my forte but my chain jumped as I went up the hill. Anne Riemersma won in 1 minute 49 seconds – my time was 1 minute 58 seconds. The first stage proper was the Fauville 'nocturne' (taking place in the evening) a 20-lap circuit race in which I rode well for the first 15 laps and even gained a 'prime' (first to the top of a hill) on lap 10, splitting the field but I lost strength in the latter part of the stage finishing 9th. Anne Riemersma won the road race part of the stage.

The next day, stage 2 was a 65 km route from Yvetot to Yerville and it poured with rain. On this hilly stage Terrie and I kept attacking to gain prime points but the Swede Pia Prim caused the most damage. Anne Riemersma punctured so the GB team worked together to try to stop her catching up again. Many of the riders punctured during this very wet stage, including Minnie Brinkhoff and Marian Bik from Holland, leaving only Petra Debruin from the Dutch team. With just 10 riders left in the field and around 3 km to go, I felt really strong. The rest of my team were at the front with me just behind. I said I felt good enough to make an attack and asked them to give me space between them so I could jump away.

I was away …. and there was daylight between me and the rest of the group. Just before the finish Petra Debruin and Arlette Lacan (Normandie) sped past me. I sat on their wheels but over-braked at the last corner and had to settle for 3rd.

The last day there were two more stages – a road race from

Allouville to Gonfreville and finishing with a criterium in Le Havre … on cobbles. The road race had wet conditions again with several winding descents on wet roads, including cobbles. I can remember one section in particular where we sped downhill into a village with cobbles and then swept to the left up another hill. I recall wondering how I had stayed upright in those conditions - we were riding so fast, I didn't have time to think about it! Even so, this stage wasn't as fast as yesterday's and our team attacked to gain more prime points. As we did the final right hand turn to climb up to Gonfreville, I was glad of bottom gear but couldn't get close enough to the front to win. Pia Prim won the stage and I was 6th. Cathy Swinnerton was 5th.

The finale was the rectangular cobbled Circuit du Bassin du Commerce in Le Havre itself and again it was wet and windy - ugh. Thankfully the organisers cut the race short due to the weather conditions. At first our team missed the break. I was able to chase to join it. The race then degenerated to a 'queuing-up' race that was fast but with little action. Minnie Brinkhoff won it, I was 5th and Cathy 6th.

The overall results were Debruin first, Prim 2nd ….. and me 3rd! There was a Queen of the Mountains prize won by Prim with Lacan 2nd and me 3rd! I took home a bottle of Chianti, which doubled up as a table lamp (which I still have).

I was delighted to meet up with my penfriend Annick, with whom I had corresponded for many years as pen-friends. She braved the cold and wet weather to watch the circuit race whilst being heavily pregnant with twins.

I was very pleased with the results. I came home more confident of my stamina and a better bike handler. Good team effort with good co-ordination – everybody was good at something.

29-7-78 Keighley Velo Plastikos Road Race

In the build up to the World Championships in Germany in 1978, I took part in a ladies road race.

This road race took place in Skipton and was 36 miles long. There was a field of 14 ladies who all stayed together for the first lap until the climb. By the time five of us reached the top, we had a break. Everyone in the break had already been chosen to compete in the 1978 World Championships in Germany: Cathy Swinnerton, Terrie Riley, Brenda Atkinson, Josie Heffernan and myself.

Over the next two laps, the break continued to extend their lead on the rest of the riders. Those in the break made a couple of attempts to drop Brenda on the climb as she was the strongest sprinter. As the break made the final left turn into the lane leading to the uphill finish just over a mile away, we encountered a herd of cows across our path.

Luckily, I was the front rider and managed to pick the best way through the animals. Realising I had an advantage I 'jumped' through the herd, getting a clean break from my group. I was on my own on the climb and rapidly 'dying'. I could hear heavy breathing behind me and Josie Heffernan passed me with only a couple of hundred yards to go. For once I used my head and sat in her slip-stream and then jumped again to beat her in the sprint for the finish. I was ecstatic … my first and only road race win!!

I was on top of the world until a few weeks later when I leaned that Josie was 3-monthls pregnant at the time. Even so, I had well and truly beaten the rest on the World Champs squad.

Chapter 7 - Lands End to John O'Groats
(Stage 2)

Preface to Stage 2 of LEJOG

My original plan had been to take a week off work each year for 3 years so I could break down my ride into manageable chunks and fully take in my experiences.

Sadly, four months after completing Stage 1 my mother died at the age of 88. She had suffered physical disabilities for many years with the last two years of her life having to endure the effects of an amputation of her left lower leg when gangrene infected it, leaving her immobile. Mum had lived her life full of optimism, kindness and always greeted everyone with a smile. She had a love of music, nature, the great outdoors and gardening to name but a few. This situation took the wind out of her sails and she also suffered several minor Strokes that led to Vascular Dementia.

As I type this, the tears are rolling down my face even though nearly 10 years have passed. I miss her so much. She has been my inspiration in the way she lived her life and the care and love she showed everyone who knew her.

I know she would have wanted me to continue this challenging ride but grief and all the paperwork involved in a funeral and sorting out her affairs took over during the following 18 months.

My Mum was Swiss and lived her life in two halves as she always held onto her family in Switzerland very closely.

So, at Easter 2011, her English family took half of her ashes to one of her favourite spots at the top of Clent hills, just outside Stourbridge and each of us sprinkled some of her ashes whilst reading out one of her letters she had sent us from several years ago, which momentarily brought her back to life through her words. The love we all felt for her was almost tangible at this site and an experience I'll never forget – it brought the whole family together more deeply than at her funeral.

In the summer of 2011 my brother, sister-in-law, and sister joined my partner and I at Mum's family home in Switzerland along with three of our cousins, Thierry, Phillipe and Michel de Choudens. Our other de Choudens cousins from South of France were not able to attend. We took the remaining ashes and spread them under one of the huge Napoleonic pine trees in our grandfather's forest. Again, each of us read one of her letters, said our own tribute and my sister sang 'Summertime' for her as her ashes joined those of her parents, brother and sister under that great tree.

Her spirit lives on in all our family and she is often spoken of with deep affection and many happy memories.

A bit of background history …..

My Swiss grandparents had lived in the Domain of Beauregard in the hillside above the town of Le Locle in the canton of Neuchatel, Switzerland, positioned very close to the border with France. Thanks to the help from my cousin Thierry de Choudens, I have learned about the family history around my mother's ancestral home. My great grandfather, Henri Richard, who was my grandmother's father was the owner of the property that also included the forest around the building. In 1893, he expanded the forest by creating the Plantation and asked to be buried there, by the two huge Napoleonic Fir trees.. (This is also where my mother's ashes were laid). Ownership of the Domain of Beauregard passed to my Grandfather whose profession had been an Inspector of Forests after he left the army. There is a forest track at a place called 'L'Escarpineau' overlooking the River Doubs, which forms the frontier between Switzerland and France named after my Grandfather – Chemin de Choudens. It is within walking distance of the family home of Beauregard.

So, it was in May 2012 that I packed my panniers again to cycle from Stourbridge to Glasgow for Stage 2 of Lands End to John O'Groats.

9 – Stourbridge to Gnosall   Distance: 30 miles

How bizarre! I stood outside my house with my pannier-laden bike about to start Stage 2 of my Lands End to John O'Groats journey. As I set off, I almost felt as though I was in a dream. I have been planning this ride for so long that it felt unreal to actually be doing it, particularly after I put the project on the 'back-burner' last year so that I could join my family to place my Mum's ashes where she wanted them – some on the Clent Hills that she loved to visit from her home in Stourbridge and some in the forest of her family home in Switzerland.

It took me several miles to accept the enormity of the days ahead and was strange to be riding that first afternoon along very familiar roads to my first stop at Gnosall, knowing I would not be going home at the end of that day. I could anticipate what would appear around every corner, as I knew the roads so well. I often found myself recalling club runs along the same lanes with Stourbridge Cycling Club … a fantastic descent here, puffing and panting up a climb, a puncture stop there and the camaraderie amongst our group.

Alone with my thoughts and the sights and sounds of nature around me, I heard loads of larks and saw the first group of swallows this year. There were frequent wafts of pungent Oilseed Rape from fields on my route with Cow Parsley, Pink Campion and clumps of Bluebells in the hedgerows.

The lanes were pretty busy and although it was misty and overcast, I could just make out 'The Wrekin' (all that's left from an ancient volcanic plug) in the direction of Telford from the top of the 'Little Clive' on my way to Pattingham. There is a 'Big Clive' within a couple of hundred yards along the same hill ridge and our cycling club used to hold the annual free-wheeling contest down it – it is a 'stinker' to climb so I opted for the more gentle 'Little Clive'.

After Pattingham and more climbing, I stopped at Boscobel House for my picnic – another often visited refreshment stop on cycling club rides. King Charles II made this house famous when he hid in an oak tree in the grounds whilst the Roundheads actually rode under the actual tree he was hiding in during the Civil War in the 17th century. He later hid in an upstairs room reserved for storing vegetables, such as onions and leeks. He was deliberately hidden there to mask his human scent when the Roundheads sent the dogs in. In those days people didn't have very good personal hygiene so the dogs would soon have found him.

After crossing the busy M54, I headed up to Bishops Wood and soon found myself in Wheaton Aston, which is about as far as I can recall going on club runs from home. My route took me through this village where I noticed an old CTC (Cyclists Touring Club) plaque on the wall. It had quite an iconic design, a little like the Isle of Man flag with three wings inside a bicycle wheel.

Feeling adventurous at Upper Cowley, I tried a short section of canal towpath on the Shropshire Union canal to Gnosall but found it rather muddy, making the going hard with a heavy weight on my bike. As I left the towpath to return to a road I looked to my left - there straight ahead was my B&B for this evening.

I had time to explore the village of Gnosall and that evening enjoyed a lovely meal at The Boat Inn alongside the canal where I spoke with a couple of people sat at other tables.

10 – Gnosall to Northwich

Looking out of the window from my B&B I saw it was pretty damp with low cloud mist – miserable in fact. A Dutch couple soon joined me at breakfast but they didn't seem to want to chat and their demeanour was quite cold. Having an open and friendly disposition, I can't help myself and have a desire to chat to my fellow guests. Later, their companions, also Dutch, joined them and soon I couldn't understand a word they said. They were visiting friends was as much as I could get out of them but I did suggest they visit Boscobel House and showed them my photo of it.

Soon I was on my way and decided to try the canal towpath again. However, my map showed I could get onto a disused railway track instead. This track is now a recognised cycle route so that I could meet the lane I needed a bit further on. It was a case of panniers off ... panniers on ... as I negotiated steps to and from the canal towpath to the railway track.

I finally got going again and soon reached Sutton where I went off my planned route to Shebdon to meet the Shropshire Union canal once again. The towpath was just grass and although it was pleasant, it was hard going and rather bumpy with the heavy load my bike was carrying – I clearly didn't learn from my first attempt. I was glad to get off by Soudley Park where I met a man with 2 friendly dogs. Again the panniers had to be removed and replaced in order to get the bike up the steps to meet the lane.

I was now on National Cycle Network Route 75 and rode through Cheswardine to Chipnall. Here I enjoyed a lovely view towards Hales and immediately had one of the best descents of the day ... followed by an inevitable climb from The Lloyd to Hales. It began to rain at this point – there was no sign of rain in the puddles by the side of the road but I could feel that very fine rain that soon soaks you to the skin.

I carried on to Bloreheath and took a photo of a pool, willow tree and bank behind it. According to my map there was a symbol of crossed swords and the date of 1459, signifying there had been a battle there. Investigating it later, it turned out to be <u>THE</u> battle that started the War of the Roses in the 15th Century: https://en.wikipedia.org/wiki/Battle_of_Blore_Heath

Arriving in Nantwich I stopped at a café and called at a Holland & Barrett shop for some provisions. The poor shop assistant was rather flustered – a lady visiting her father's neighbour had met his dog, which had jumped up and bitten the lady's coat, creating a small bite mark. The lady had gone berserk at the shop assistant's father, telling him he would have to replace the coat, which cost £120!

Back on my bike and just after Wettenhall I needed to answer a call of nature in a field. As I squatted down I saw a delightful scene of dandelion 'clocks' full of seeds and grasses with beads of water droplets from the morning's rain – I went back for my camera!

My plan was to meet up with my great cycle-racing friend Faith Murray at Winsford and I had phoned her earlier to let her know where I was. I turned a corner by the Salt Mines and there she was, having ridden out to meet me. It felt wonderful to be in her company again; she set a cracking pace and I struggled to keep up on my heavily laden bike. At Bradford Mill we came off the lane and went down to meet the Weaver Navigation, riding along the towpath to her home in Northwich. It was a very wide river and straight too as it had been artificially changed to accommodate the larger boats.

Soon we went over Vale Royal Locks and then crossed the Blue Bridge back down the other side to the newly made pathway that was wide enough for us to ride 2-abreast. We passed the rowing club that Faith is involved with and over another lock crossing to come out in a housing estate that led to her home (meeting her son Iain and dog 'Stig' on the way). Here we had a proper greeting with her husband David too. Soon we were chatting over a drink and cake, catching up with several years-worth of gossip.

After a lovely meal with the family, Faith and I chatted till gone 11 pm, reminiscing about our shared cycle-racing experiences and many of the people and other competitors we both knew. She was enjoying her work as a Chiropodist and spoke with pride about her daughter Sian and son Iain. We could have gone on chatting all night but sleep beckoned.

11 – Northwich to Ainsworth   Distance: 37 miles

After breakfast chatting with Faith and David and looking through the wedding photos of their daughter, it was time for me to set off. I loaded up my bike and took a photo of them in their garden. Faith rode with me as far as the Lidl store, getting me to the High Marston Road out of Northwich.

*****

Faith and I met at the World Cycling Championships in Varese, Italy in 1971. She was taking part in the sprint, which was her forte (she won the Ladies National Sprint title six years on the trot!) I took part in both the sprint and road race at this Championship event but sadly I was nowhere near ready for international competition and the experience nearly put me off cycling altogether.

Over the years Faith and I rode together many times, mainly at track events, a few time trials and also in road races. We used to meet up regularly on a Wednesday evening taking part in Salford Track League in Erdington, Birmingham – directly underneath 'Spaghetti Junction'. The track is no longer there now and the area has become a football ground. We used to have a lot of fun together, becoming great friends and supporting each other in our separate disciplines.

One of my favourite memories is when we had travelled south together to ride the Ladies National 25-mile Time Trial and we stayed with a friend of my Mum's. We rode the Time Trial the next morning and took the opportunity to ride an Open Track Meeting in Reading (my birthplace) in the afternoon. There were some events for women so Faith and I took part in the Ladies Omnium, which was a series of

3 events that accumulated points. There was another lady called Jayne Westbury - local girl to Reading – she was one of Faith's major sprinting adversaries. The events comprised a sprint, a points race and a pursuit. Faith and I decided to work together so, in the sprint I 'boxed in' Jayne to prevent her chasing when Faith attacked, Faith and I took it in turns during the points race and I won the pursuit. We were delighted! However, we were reprimanded by the officials from Reading track for 'working over' their local girl and were 'banned' from riding there again!

That kind of behaviour happens all the time in the men's races and its considered 'good tactics' .... but not 'acceptable' for ladies !!!!! It is a story I love telling ... so full of mischief. It also demonstrated the sexist behaviour towards women participating in cycle racing at that time (1970's). I doubt the likes of Laura Kenny and Lizzie Armistead would tolerate such treatment today. I feel very proud to have been one of the original trailblazers to push forward women's cycle racing during my era when it was definitely considered the 'Cinderella' of sports.

Faith and I would always get changed into more feminine clothes after racing and made a point of looking quite glamorous. When we reappeared at the track centre there were often remarks of: 'We didn't recognise you with clothes on'! Cheeky fellows!

After our racing careers ended and our children came into our lives, we still used to meet up around once a year and, as is often the way with close friends, it always felt as though we had only seen each other the week before and we'd be chatting and laughing together.

Little did I know this would be the last time I would ever see Faith. She died from a fluke heart attack just after Christmas 2013. Such a fit lady, still being active both in cycling and rowing. Her daughter had been in the Junior International Squad in rowing and Faith had become deeply involved in Northwich Rowing Club. In fact, on Boxing Day 2013, she had been coxing some of the events for their annual event. The following morning, her husband David had gone downstairs to make them both a cup of tea and when he came back, she'd had a severe heart attack and never came round again. Their family was devastated! I still find it hard to come to terms that she is gone.

*****

I continued my route to Ainsworth, near Bury. Soon I rejoined the designated cycle route at Great Budworth. I stopped to check my map and a group of cyclists from Chester CTC passed me – on a car-assisted ride to Alderley Edge. I caught them up and chatted with a man at the back of the group who turned out to know some cycling friends near where I live, Kevin and Sue Payton, having ridden with them at the Tour Federale in France - small world. I rode with the group over the M6 to Crossroads Farm where they turned right and I carried on towards Lymm. The weather was still rather cold and miserable today so I was glad to be wearing plenty of layers.

The terrain was very flat so I made good time and at Warburton I went across the Toll Bridge over the Manchester Ship Canal, which was an impressive landmark. I then rode through Glazebrook and the outskirts of Culcheth where I began to get into the built up suburbs of Leigh. At Bedford I got onto the Bridgwater Canal towpath, which had a cinder surface and was so much quieter than the roads. Riding along canal towpaths near my home I am used to the feeling of figuratively going through the door in the wardrobe, Narnia-style, as the two travel-ways are like moving between totally different dimensions. There is all the hustle and bustle of road traffic and suddenly, within a matter of yards along a canal towpath, it is a different and more tranquil world. I got off at Ashley Green where I chatted to a family who were familiar with the area and it's coalmining history. The man told me it had been a very busy mining area with at least 6 pit-heads nearby.

I found a bridle path to Boothstown and was very pleased with myself having navigated to join a road that was on my planned route ... until I found myself by a motorway junction a couple of miles further on. I didn't check the map and had gone off course in the wrong direction. Getting myself out of predicaments caused by mistakes, as in this situation, is all part of the rich diversity of life that helps to strengthen resolve, build resilience and give a sense of achievement.

At Farnsworth I had my only incident with a motorist - the

only one of the whole LEJOG. Needless to say it was a large black 'Chelsea Tractor' whose driver seemed to think I would vanish into thin air as we encountered each other at a staggered junction. I reached the junction first and was already crossing it when he approached from my right wanting to cross my path and head to my left. He obviously hadn't seen me or hadn't anticipated my speed accurately so when he was inches from me I shouted 'Oouuii' and he had to swerve abruptly to miss me! The fact that I wore a bright yellow tabard seemed to be totally lost on this motorist.

Soon I was on my way to Little Lever having crossed a junction that I expected to be more difficult with heavy traffic. From there it was easy to reach Ainsworth except that for the first time in miles the gradient went uphill and turned out to be the steepest and longest hill of the ride so far.

I reached the top of the hill at Ainsworth where I was staying with friends Barbara and Peter Jespson, who I have known for many years and have visited them at Ainsworth many times before. I turned left … no, that didn't look right, so I retraced and went right …no that didn't look right either. It had been around 20 years since I had last visited them here and I became confused, as I had approached it from an unfamiliar direction. I started to ask people, getting various answers, ending up heading towards Bury. In the end I resorted to phoning Barbara for directions.

It was great to see them again after so long. They also had their grandchildren, Jessica and Daniel with them for the day. Jessica and I really hit it off big time and we all sat and watched the finish of the stage of the cycle stage race Giro D'Italia before Barbara announced that it was tea time.

After tea we took the children across to the park that I remember taking my sons Alex and Vincent to all those years ago. When we got back I read several stories to Jessica whilst Barbara read to Daniel before taking them upstairs for a bath. I joined her and we had fun with them both splashing around with toys before Barbara took them to bed.

Barbara, Pete and I chatted a bit longer – Pete had just turned 70 and that was why they had taken a holiday to Portugal a few weeks earlier.

12 Ainsworth to High Bentham   Distance: 51 miles

A certain little lady woke me at 6.30 am! We read some books for a while and then I got all my stuff packed and went downstairs for breakfast. I did 'wake up' Laughter Yoga with the children and wished Pete a belated Happy Birthday.

Soon I loaded up the bike, said my 'thank you's' and was on my way – Pete, having looked at my route, said I would have a hard ride to High Bentham today (he proved only too right).

It was a lovely sunny morning with low clouds hugging the tops of the moors but it was very cold so I had plenty of layers on. I set off towards Tottington and immediately the road began to climb … on and on and on. It continued after I turned left onto Watling Street through Affetride and Edgeworth. Then the climbing really started and I found myself in my very lowest gear more frequently than I'd expected. On and on it climbed but I was being rewarded by great views. I was actually climbing Holcombe Moor!

What goes up must come down and I had a brilliant long descent into Blackburn. Thankfully, I'd identified a route to bypass most of the town, which didn't look particularly inviting.

Soon I was climbing out of the town towards Sunny Bower and my mobile phone rang. I stopped near the top of a hill and rummaged in my top bag to get to the phone, which immediately stopped ringing as I put my hands on it! I returned the call, which was in response to an email I'd sent from home before I left. The person I'd sent it to had inadvertently deleted it and wanted me to re-send it. Thankfully, I was able to locate my message from my mobile and simply re-sent it. The wonders of modern technology – otherwise they would have had to wait until I returned home.

Back in the saddle, I climbed up towards Rishton and at last re-joined a cycle route that is part of the LEJOG route recommended by the CTC (Cycling UK). The climb went through a village called York and then I had a tremendous descent into the Ribble Valley, into a town called Whalley where there were fantastic views including a most impressive railway viaduct. Soon I was in for a treat as Pendle Hill came into view just by Mitton Hall Hotel.

I stopped for lunch in a field and became aware I didn't have much water left and the weather had become so hot I had removed several layers, now riding in shorts. Soon I began to start a long climb at Cow Ark. As I turned a corner, I was lucky enough to find a couple in their garden and asked them to refill my water bottle. I was most grateful and it was spring water too.

Now for the climb up Birker Fell. What an absolute treat. The views were stunning so needless to say I kept stopping to take photos. Being in such a remote place, all on my own and being able to just soak up the raw natural beauty all around me was utter bliss. I had just taken a photo of a forest with gorgeous views beyond it and I could see the road would then go on a descent.

Wow … what a roller-coaster! What a corker! Talk about exhilarating!! As I was freewheeling down, gravity and the impetus of my heavy bike took over and I felt as though I was flying. At the bottom, I was going so fast, I was able to coast half way up the other side before pedalling again. The photo I took looking back didn't do it justice and I'm amazed I managed to stay upright – I didn't have time to think that I could have fallen off. If I had the opportunity, would I do it again? …. Absolutely!

There followed another descent all the way down to Newton and then I found I was only 2 miles from Slaidburn so, as I was far too early to continue to High Bentham, I took the opportunity to stop at the 'Hark to Bounty' pub in the village where I sat in the sunshine with a cool drink and wrote up my diary. There was only another 11 miles further to ride to High Bentham. A stroll in the park …. me thought.

As I set off, the road became yet another roller-coaster. Soon there was a descent through some threes and then … it loomed up in front of me – Lythe Fell and Burn Moor - part of the Forest of Bowland. I gulped at the realisation. The bottom of the climb reminded me of Holme Moss from the Glossop side so I knew I was in for a long slog - so much for my complacency at Slaidburn!

Putting the bike into absolute bottom gear, I set about a very slow ascent that took around 30 minutes. It was so remote with sheep looking like tiny dots on the landscape – one of those weird tricks of the mind when the scene in front of you is so vast; it's difficult to get a sense of scale. I hadn't quite reached the top when I stopped to take a photo looking back the way I'd come (and wished I'd thought to take a photo at the bottom first!).

I finished the climb in cloudy weather and there was another 5 miles to do. It was a terrific descent back into sunshine with fantastic views – I squinted to see if I could make out High Bentham in the distance. Then it became a real roller-coaster again over streams and sometimes going back up hill again until the next long descent all the way down a sharp downhill where again, I gained sufficient impetus to get me more than half way up the other side.

Finally, I arrived at The Black Horse at High Bentham at 6.40 pm and the proprietor helped me put my bike in their shed. The 'hard ride' Pete predicted had certainly lived up to it's reputation! There were 2 other cyclists staying at the pub who were just on their way to get their meal at the pub opposite. An hour later I wandered over to the Coach House where I found the other 2 cyclists – David and Emir – known as 'M'. We had a couple of drinks together and then I joined them for a meal that finished with the most scrumptious

Sticky Toffee Pudding I've ever had (loads of treacle). We came back to the Black Horse pub for another drink and joined in with the quiz that was going on.

13 High Bentham to Lazonby   Distance: 58 miles

I joined David and 'M' at breakfast and we chatted about our routes for the day – they were going in the opposite direction to me today.

With my bike loaded up for the day, I quickly went to the shop for provisions and, as I looked in my bum-bag, realised I'd left my iPhone in my room and the proprietor of the Black Horse pub had already gone out to take her mother to hospital. I was in a real panic as I'd no idea how long she would take and I had around 60-miles to ride ahead of me.

I went in search for a member of staff but all was quiet. I tried the back door and it was open. Thankfully, I remembered the keypad code to gain access to the accommodation part of the pub. I gingerly pushed my door and, with a great sense of relief, found I had not fully closed it so it hadn't locked! I retrieved my iPhone and charger. Phew ….. lesson learned.

It was a glorious day and already warm enough to be in shorts and short-sleeved top. I'd only ridden a little way out when I glanced to my right and saw magnificent Ingleborough Hill in all its glory. Crossing a main road, I then went through Ireby to Cowan Bridge where I'd planned to ride along a disused railway line but it had all but disappeared. I joined the main road into Kirkby Lonsdale, which was a pretty place with lots of local stone buildings – I would have loved to take more photos in the centre with all its interesting architecture but the view was spoiled by a very busy car park. Leaving Kirkby Lonsdale I took a delightful leafy lane and, as I descended a hill, I caught the scent of bluebells, which duly appeared as I turned a corner – what a sight. It was all the more enticing as I could also look across the River Lune towards Barbon and hills beyond.

Further on, I got rather concerned about a dog I heard barking in a field as it was tied up and in full sun. I tried to give it some water but it shied away from me. Eventually I found the farmer who owned it and voiced my concerns. I hope it was OK when the farmer found it.

The lane towards Sedburgh was a delight, quiet and sometimes narrow, surrounded by spring vegetation and dramatic hills. I felt in my element, full of the joy I felt from just being out in nature and being able to fully appreciate it, a huge grin on my face.

Setting off from Sedburgh after a lunch stop, I headed towards Howgill and was able to look back at the route I had just come along. Ahead of me was an extremely undulating stretch of road – absolutely no flat. I was mostly in my lowest gear to get up the steep inclines. The views more than compensated as I rode towards Fell Head. It was also quite strange to hear the M6 motorway and eventually to see vehicles on it heading up Shap Fell, particularly as I approached Low Boroughbridge. Here I also saw a high-speed train and wondered whether this might be my route home by train on Sunday (it was!).

Soon I crossed over the motorway and headed for Tebay, pleased with myself for taking a useful short cut to Orton. The trouble was I didn't check my map properly and went to Gaisgill instead of Old Tebay so added a couple of miles to get to Orton. I stopped here for an ice cream and was very grateful to sit beside a couple of locals who, on checking my planned route, realised I would have made a very costly mistake a few miles further on.

I climbed out of Orton up a very steep but short hill and was fascinated with the changing geology at Orton Seat where the hills were quite definitely limestone, whereas the hills previously had been a much harder, rugged rock.

I then took a gated road on my left heading for Crosby Ravensworth and was preparing myself for another hard ride when I was rewarded instead with a tremendous descent into a pretty, leafy valley. This road was gently undulating and with a tailwind – I could easily ride at 14 mph as I rode to Maulds Meaburn and Kings Meaburn. I continued to Temple Sowerby where I recognised some of the hills in the distance from riding the C2C (Coast to Coast between Tynemouth to Whitehaven) with my partner, Steve in 2003 and wondered whether one of them was 'Hartside'. The mere mention of 'Hartside' would bring out a chorus or 'urghh's' from cyclists having made its acquaintance – a long, hard slog on the A686 over the Pennine Hills.

I rode on to Lazonby via Langwathby, bringing back more memories when Steve and I stayed there when we rode the C2C. As I rode the last few miles, I was conscious that a slight wind had come up – nice and cooling but actually against me. I reached Lazonby and stopped at the Co-op to buy food so that I could cook my evening meal – the landlady at my B&B told me that the pub down the road would not do meals that evening so she allowed me to make use of her kitchen. She greeted me as I arrived and helped me with my panniers into her delightful 17th century house that was full of character – Mum would have loved it.

I went downstairs after settling into my room and cooked my meal whilst chatting with the landlady who also agreed to put some of my clothes through the washing machine. We had a lovely chat and I felt very much at home with her and her husband.

14 Lazonby to Moffat   Distance: 64 miles

I was grateful for a glorious morning. With a long ride ahead of me, including crossing into Scotland, I loaded my bike and was away early

I had quite a climb out of Lazonby and my legs felt quite sluggish so I didn't rush too much to give my legs the chance to gradually lose all yesterday's lactic acid. As I rode through lanes the scenery was gorgeous with rich green spring foliage everywhere and occasionally I saw signs depicting red squirrels by woods where they lived but warned motorists to take care against them becoming 'road kill'. Sadly I didn't see any but felt gladdened to know they are protected locally.

Through a valley to my left I could just make out the Lakeland peaks as the heat haze made visibility poor. Periodically I had views of a railway line (it had passed through Lazonby too) – this was the Settle to Carlisle line.

On the approach to Carlisle I made my way to the centre to have a quick look around. Near the Tourist Office, I was amused to see road signs for ' Scotch Street' and English Street' right next to each other.

A lot of the centre was pedestrianised and there were all the usual 'names' amongst the shops. I found the Cathedral, which I visited before with Steve when we did the C2C in 2003 but wanted to see it again. As I took a photo of it from the gateway, a man pointed out a gargoyle at the end nearest the gate - it was a policeman's head, complete with helmet! Going inside, I wanted to see the spectacular ceiling again. A deep royal blue with gold coloured partitions making the roof an arch of squares, it's absolutely stunning all along the nave.

I left Carlisle along the dual carriageway that passed the castle and found well signed shared-use pedestrian and cycle paths. I followed them to cross the bridge over the River Eden and then climbed through a residential area to a left turn at a set of traffic lights and was soon out in the country on a lane, heading west.

Soon I approached a large roundabout at a new junction signposted to Cargo and Rockcliffe. Thanks to Steve's research, this was the junction I needed to reach the road to cross the River Esk that led into Scotland. I soon passed Cargo and then turned left into the village of Rockcliffe. A bit further on I saw a signpost to Gretna and then, after a 10-minute stop at a level crossing for 4 trains (I would cross it by train on my homeward journey), there was the sign to Metal Bridge and Gretna. I then turned left on to a lane that ran beside the A74M (M6) across the River Esk.

The terrain was pretty flat here and there was a brisk crosswind as I made my way to Gretna Green, stopping by the 'Welcome to Scotland' sign opposite the Old Smithy's Marriage Rooms, famous for people absconding to get married. I was in Scotland! I felt I had really achieved a milestone.

By now I was pretty hungry and set off into the small village to find some food. I found a line of shops that included a marriage Registry Office and there I found a bakery. I mentioned to one of the assistants that I was on my way to Moffatt and she recommended 'Brodie's' for my evening meal – I later took up her recommendation.

I set off and was soon riding alongside the A74M again along the A7076. This was the main road until the motorway superseded it. I was still heading west at this point with the pesky crosswind.

As I looked back I could only just make out the Lakeland Fells and saw a strange phenomenon of a layer of fog over the estuary of the Solway Firth. It reminded me of a similar sight at Akureyri in Iceland where a strip of fog hung half way between the top and bottom of a mountain, giving it quite an eerie atmosphere.

It didn't take me long to reach Lockerbie as I began to head north-west and kept criss-crossing the A74M. There was constant road noise but the surface was good and very little traffic on the A7076. I deviated into the town of Lockerbie to have a look around and perhaps find a memorial to the devastation caused by Pan-Am Flight 103 in 1988 as it blew up over the town due to a terrorist bomb on board. I was unable to find the memorial so I continued on my route along the A7076 again. The weather had become very hot and muggy and I watched growing clouds with suspicion in case they turned into cumulonimbus!

Soon I reached Johnstonbridge and over to the right the scenery began looking more interesting with some mountains looming up. I had been making fast progress on this road, keeping 13-14 mph but it had become very boring and the constant road noise from the motorway alongside me grated on my ears. I stopped to check my map and found I could turn off to Newton a few miles further on and approach Moffatt from a lane that practically ran parallel but some distance away. What a difference! It was immediately more tranquil and closer to the foothills. I had only another 6 miles to Moffatt and thoroughly enjoyed this last section.

I approached the town along the Old Carlisle Road and soon Rosebery House appeared on my right and I'd arrived early evening having ridden 64.11 miles! Jan, the lady of the house showed me to my room. The view from it was gorgeous and the room itself was spacious – I could have had a party in the en-suite bathroom – it was huge! The only problem was the climb of 40 steps to reach it!

Later, I walked into the town on rather wobbly legs to find something to eat and found 'Brodie's' restaurant (thanks to the lady at Gretna) where I had a fantastic meal. At first I thought it wouldn't fill me as it was rather a 'foodie' type of place but the dishes were deceptive. The proprietor also sponsored me when I explained what I was doing on my ride.

Afterwards, I had a quick walk around the town, which was delightful and I will look around further tomorrow. I investigated Well Street and found a plaque on the wall about Robert the Bruce and then walked back to Rosebery House.

15 Moffat to Lanark   Distance: 40 miles

Waking quite early this morning I saw a heavy, low fog outside the window. So different from the view seen from there last night – now I couldn't see the houses 50 metres away! As time passed, sunlight gradually started to burn through and I saw part of the fog had lifted with a cloud hanging in the balance between the ground and the top of the hill beyond. It was a very similar phenomenon that happens at my mother's family home in the Swiss Jura or by rivers as the fog evaporates.

Soon Jan, my landlady, arrived to make breakfast and as she busied herself in the kitchen we had a chat about anything that came into our heads and our respective families. She gave me a good idea to pass on – when her children misbehaved, she sat them on chairs back-to-back and gave them a time limit of 10-15 minutes to change their behaviour to 'angels' before she'd allow them to get down. They once had to sit like that for an hour – they never pushed her that far again! She gave me a lovely breakfast and we got on so well I was reluctant to leave.

The weather was bright and warm again as I set off into Moffat for a look around before I left. I was concerned about my back tyre, which was a bit soft and went in search of a bike shop. I was told about 'Moffat Can' – a community project that does all sorts of things and might have a better bicycle pump than my little one. I was fascinated by their set-up – recycling cans, paper, plastic, cooking oil to make into bio-fuel to run their van, etc. They also have a super allotment that they only started 2 years ago that included a composting plant and hot-house run by solar panels and solar thermal with a very expensive-looking machine that does all sorts of conversions. They also keep fish (a kind of carp) that they breed and allow to grow before selling to local restaurants. As it is rich in nitrates, the 'waste' from the fish is added to the compost. I was most impressed and told them about 'Dudley Greenagers' a project within Age UK Dudley where I worked. They changed my tyre and after giving them a donation, I set off to re-join the cycle route alongside the A74M.

The terrain was becoming hillier now and I found myself on a long gradual climb. This must have gone on for around 10 miles before the odd downhill and then climbing again, with scenery that was pleasant but very much same as, same as.

Then I saw some wind turbines – the further I rode, the more I saw. They were high up in the hills on both sides of the road – there seemed to be hundreds of them – the most I'd ever seen in one place. I loved watching them move so gracefully, providing energy through the wind's natural resource.

I came across a works entrance stating that the turbines are part of the Upper Clyde Wind Farm. There was a barrier across the cycle path to the works entrance (similar to canal towpath barriers). At that point there was a workman beside his truck and I asked him who was responsible for putting up barriers that are such a nuisance to cyclists as it meant having to dismount and remount to negotiate the barriers. He was a friendly Welsh workman from the Rhondda Valley and we had a light-hearted chat about the logic and intelligence of local councils 'making sure they adhere to health & safety'. He then told me a steam train was due to pass by. The main train line from Glasgow to Carlisle ran between the road I was on and the A74M – this was the same line I would travel home on. I hadn't ridden much further when the steam train appeared and I fumbled for my camera, just catching a shot of it as it passed by – I think it was 'The Mallard'.

It felt as though I would never reach Abington, the next village along the route but I enjoyed catching glimpses of the young River Clyde winding through the valley. It felt strange to think that by the end of tomorrow, I would reach Glasgow having followed the course of this magnificent river, through its gorge at Lanark to where the docks meet the sea.

After Abington, I had the choice of continuing on the same road or taking a detour along a road that would meet up with my original road about 6 miles further on. I chose the 'scenic route' on the B7078. There were miles of moorland and hardly any habitation all around me as I cycled. It was incredibly remote and I was glad to have perfect weather, as it could have felt very lonely and sinister in less clement weather. It actually felt more remote than cycling over Dartmoor. I felt so privileged to find myself in such an area of complete natural beauty, totally alone but at ease.

The scenic route returned to being close to the A74M at the junction just before Happendon services. Soon I was riding towards Douglas Water through some woods on an undulating lane that felt harder than I expected, my knees were all but buckling from several steep uphill gradients.

Then I could see Lanark – perched on top of a ridge and reminding me of the fabulous view of Toledo in central Spain (but that was much grander). Unfortunately, there was a long descent to Kirkfieldbank followed by a long climb to get me back to the same height I was before the descent! The ascent to Lanark itself was so steep, I rode up it very slowly in my lowest gear. Towards the top there was a road junction where a queue of traffic was forming. Struggling up this steep hill, I was grateful the traffic began moving again, as I would not have been able to get going again if I'd had to stop. I soon arrived at this evening's B&B but was earlier than expected. I got the impression my landlady was not pleased as she was in the middle of putting up some garden decorations.

My room was very small compared to the last 2 places I'd stayed at but was clean and pleasant. I walked back into the town to find somewhere to have my supper. Eventually I found 'Prego', an Italian restaurant and ordered my meal. I had just started eating when another lady on her own came in – a similar situation to my visit to

Plymouth 2 years ago. I invited her to join me. She had recently moved into a new home in Lanark having come from Cumbernauld, just outside Glasgow. We had a fascinating evening together chatting about all sorts. She used to deliver presentations and a bit of lecturing and then had several years caring for her husband and elderly relatives. As I would be going to Glasgow, she suggested I visit the People's Palace at Glasgow Green when I reach there tomorrow. We parted as the best of friends having spent a most enjoyable evening together.

16 Lanark to Glasgow   Distance: 35 miles

Nice room and breakfast but the landlady was still rather distant – quite a contrast to Jan at Moffat yesterday. However, when I asked her to sign my LEJOG record card, she softened and only asked me for £30, giving me £5.00 for my sponsorship.

I left early and headed straight for the World Heritage Site at New Lanark on a glorious morning. It was quite a long descent to New Lanark and that gave me concern for riding back up as my legs still felt pretty tired from yesterday's ride. The visitor centre wasn't open yet but there was nothing stopping me wandering around the village so I looked around and was drawn by a water wheel and the sound of a waterfall and weir on the River Clyde alongside the village. As I explored I saw signs to 'Cora Linn Falls' along a woodland path beside the road and went along to explore.

Soon I found myself walking along a wooden boardwalk at the water's edge and woodland where labels had been stuck in the ground next to various wild flowers, including Water Avens. I came to the Hydro-Electric station in a building that looked slightly similar to the water pumping stations along the canals near home and a huge, long pipework leading from upstream into the plant. I continued beyond and climbed a winding path from where I could hear the thundering of falling water. I climbed a little further and turned a corner and there was Cora Linn in the most delightful setting. It was stunning and almost moved me to tears. I love to be amongst nature and to be so close to this tremendous force of natural power was truly awesome.

I took some photos and started my return trip, meeting a couple en route. The man had a stick and limped so he stayed below the last flight of steps whilst his wife went to see the falls from the viewpoint whilst I chatted to him. He was 80 and suffering from a back problem. His wife was French and they spend a lot of time in La Rochelle. This place is a favourite haunt for them both but sadly he can no longer reach the viewpoint.

Back at the World Heritage Site of cotton mills at New Lanark, I was fascinated to learn about this feature of the Industrial Revolution and in particular, Robert Owen, who was a businessman and social activist. As one of the textile mill owners here, he improved the living conditions and education of his workers. He set the blueprint for education of working class people across the UK.

Returning to my bike, I started the long haul back up into Lanark and from Kirkfieldbank I could see a tremendous view to the hills beyond Lanark in the direction I travelled yesterday. I took a left turn along a narrow lane (that I nearly missed) that descended into Crossford. Here I joined a busy, narrow road with heavy traffic and I couldn't find anywhere to stop to check my map. Consequently, I missed my turning off it but was eventually able to take a turn off to Larkfield.

Here I stopped to buy a huge sandwich at a shop that obviously catered for all the local businesses, which although very busy was friendly and efficient. I then turned onto a lane that went downhill quite steeply and couldn't resist stopping at a pub at the bottom for a drink. Unfortunately, I then had a stinker of a climb immediately afterwards. From the top I could see some tall flats in the distance and presumed these were at Hamilton.

Reaching the main road, I soon found myself in the suburbs of Hamilton. I felt quite pleased with myself for working out this route on the Landranger map as it kept me off the busy roads and mainly through residential areas.

Soon I reached Flemington and occasionally could see impressive views across the Glasgow conurbation but none were good enough to take a photo – I could even see some impressive mountains beyond.

My mapping again proved very helpful and at High Crosshall, I found another cycle route that took me through a park and residential roads and then alongside a dual carriageway until at last it took me through a lovely park that led to a footbridge over a now very mature River Clyde.

Soon I was riding along the riverside on a designated path and cycleway in the same way it would be possible to ride along London's Embankment. I also rode through the bottom of Glasgow Green (a bit like Hyde Park) and realised I was very close to the People's Palace that my companion at Lanark mentioned last night. I promised myself to visit again tomorrow without the bike.

After riding underneath the motorway along the waterside, I followed signs heading for Kevlingrove Museum + Art Gallery as the Youth Hostel was nearby. A couple of wrong turnings and one last climb and I was there – journey's end!

I felt a mixture of relief and regret that my adventure for this stage was over but most of all I wanted to 'stop'. I put my bike into the Youth Hostel store and took all my stuff to a 6-bedded ladies dormitory.

The building is a 3-storey Edwardian townhouse that wouldn't look out of place in one of the crescents in Cheltenham or Bath and painted brilliant white. Inside there was a beautiful panelled staircase that gave an indication of its former grandeur.

Later, I went for a walk in Kelvingrove Park. It was a scorching afternoon of 23°C and the park was crowded the sun-bathers and families cooking BBQ's. It was like being on a seaside beach! Whilst walking in the park and chatting to Steve on my mobile phone to tell him I'd arrived, I saw 2 girls with a pair of ferrets on leads and was allowed to stroke one of them – how cute.

Rest Day and 7-mile walk around Glasgow

I chatted to 2 other ladies in my dormitory this morning and had breakfast with one of them who was from Colorado - here for a weekend course at the Conservatoire learning how to direct a show.

After breakfast I set off on foot for the day, through Kelvingrove Park towards the Museum and Art Gallery. The park was very quiet this morning after so many people enjoying yesterday's sunshine. The entrance hall was huge and looked more like the nave of a wide cathedral with an organ at the far end. I went into a room of model animals – from elephants, giraffes, etc to a spider crab. Up above these models was a Spitfire aeroplane!

I wondered through various halls and was amazed by the Expressionists Gallery where about 40 white polystyrene 'heads' were suspended from the ceiling with various expressions on their faces. I found a couple of Monet paintings and learned that he had difficulty capturing the light in Mediterranean landscapes. There was a religious 'Dali' painting of Christ on the cross but from the perspective from above – apparently, Dali had 2 dreams that led him to paint this together with an older sketch by another artist.

Having spent a good hour looking around I then set off towards the River Clyde. Then, I had a brainwave to do a 'recky' to find Central Station, from which I shall take my train home tomorrow. At Central Station I found I would have to use the lift to reach the correct platform with my loaded bike. The station was packed with people and had shops and eateries similar to what I would find at Victoria Station in London.

Afterwards I walked down to the path beside the River Clyde and soon reached Glasgow Green – not as busy as it had been yesterday and I made my way to the People's Palace where I was able to buy a baguette for my lunch. The two ladies at Larkhall would have been horrified at the pathetic specimen I was presented with! Nevertheless, I took it outside and as I was eating, 2 ladies asked to join me at my table. They were old college friends who meet up from time to time.

Afterwards I had a look around the Hot-House and then at the exhibits that my companion told me about whilst at Lanark. I was so grateful for her suggestion, as it was well worth looking at to see how people lived in the tenement buildings and also the active suffragette movement, the way the workers revolted to get better working conditions and the fortunes made by entrepreneurs during the Industrial Revolution.

I began to set off back down the riverbank to the hostel as it was already after 3.00 pm. I headed west first before I could cross the 'Squidgy Bridge' – a modern bridge with an attractive arc over it. I then made my way up to climb towards the hostel, passing 2 strange churches nearby.

Despite having cycled many miles to reach here from Stourbridge, by the time I got to the Youth Hostel I was absolutely drained from such a long walk and walking slowly around the museum – my feet were so sore!

Soon afterwards, the lady I spoke to this morning in my dormitory came returned and we had a lovely chat – she was buzzing from her course and is delighted she's learned so much.

I went downstairs to have my evening meal. An Australian lady was having a meal too so we chatted across the tables. She is half way through a protracted visit to the UK, visiting places and meeting people to help her trace her family tree. She will also be visiting places in the Midlands, including Lichfield, Bromsgrove, Hereford and Ludlow. With another 10 weeks in Britain it has quite obviously taken over her life as she tries to piece together a large family and their activities in World War 2 in particular.

The next day I took the train back from Glasgow to Wolverhampton. It felt so strange passing places I'd cycled along only a few days earlier, particularly along the Lune Valley where both the M6 and the railway line run through on their way up Shap Fell. I reminisced how lucky I was to be able to take in the sights I passed through at a much more leisurely pace.

Photos from Stage 2

Boscobel House – where King Charles II hid

Dandelion with raindrops – Wettenhall

Faith and David Murray – Northwich

Holcombe Moor - approaching Blackburn

Pendle Hill from a tributary of River Ribble

Descent from Mart Hill Moor - the photo doesn't do it justice! I started at the descent from the corner by the tree and 'flew' along this roller coaster

Looking back down climb on Lythe Fell and Burn Moor on the way
to High Bentham

Lune Valley and M6 Motorway heading towards Shap Fell

77

Signpost in Carlisle – Scotch Street and English Street

Marriage Rooms at Gretna Green

Cora Linn – Falls of Clyde at New Lanark

Glasgow Youth Hostel – end of Stage 2

79

Chapter 8 - Nationals and World Championships 1978

Amongst several road races I rode, I was disappointed with my position of 4th in the National Road Race at Sutton Bonnington, ignoring an opportunity close to the finish. Brenda Atkinson won, Denise Burton was second and Cathy Swinnerton just beat me to the bronze medal.

However, I was delighted to win the Ladies National Pursuit Championship for the second year, proving that my 1977 win was not just a 'one-off'. I had stiff competition from Brenda Atkinson and Denise Burton. Throughout, the three of us were very close in the times we recorded and the fastest I recorded was 4.14.45 with Brenda breathing down my neck with a fastest of 4.14.55. By the time we reached the finals, I beat Brenda 4.16.57 to her 4.22.41. Denise took the bronze medal with 4.17.57 beating Cathy Swinnerton with 4.21.96.

After my disappointments at the World Championships in 1977, this whole season had been geared in preparation to make improvements at the World Championships in Munich (track) and Cologne (road). I had consistently improved in strength, skill and confidence throughout the 1978 season and relished the thought of getting through the preliminaries at the World Pursuit Championships.

Here follows what happened ….

What could be safer than sitting on the wheel of the Canadian, Karen Strong. Last year she won the bronze medal in the pursuit at San Cristobel, Venezuela - she was steady as a rock to follow. No problem.

We were warming up - the final five minute twiddle on the Munich velodrome. The wooden track was an engineering masterpiece with 'G' forces on the banking that literally threw you into the next straight.

Butterflies were fluttering as if there was a swarm of them in my stomach but I felt full of confidence and I knew I'd done all the preparation. I was ready to take on the likes of Keetie Van Ousten Hage and the rest of the world. Sat comfortably on the wheel of Karen Strong - the blond bombshell from Canada - I felt nothing could stop me doing the ride of my life.

Suddenly, I felt as if I was being swallowed by a hole in the ground. I looked up and I could see the sky and the roof that covered the spectators. I was lying at the track edge, midway round the banking. What happened?

Officials were running towards me from all directions, my bike was taken from me. Val Rushworth, the Ladies National Coach sat me down and asked if I was hurt. Where had my bike gone - I wanted to get back on - the five-minute warm-up period was nearly over. I NEEDED to get back on!

Too late. The Ladies World Pursuit Championship preliminary heats had started. Shaken, angry and my confidence shattered, all I could do was warm up in the track centre. WHY had I fallen off? There was nothing wrong with my bike. Andy, my husband, managed to persuade officials not to mess around with my bike. But WHY had I fallen off?

Brenda Atkinson was on the track riding her heat - she was onto a smashing ride. My turn next. Val Rushworth helped me up to my starting station. 'Go for it Maggie, you'll do an even better ride', she whispered in my ear as I sat psyching myself for the final countdown of 'beeps' before 'take off'.

Beep, beep, beep, beep, beep, beeeeep! Out of the saddle and lunge at those pedals. Stay out of the saddle to reach optimum revs - got to get a good start.

What!

I sat down half-way round the first banking - I should have stayed out of the saddle all the way round the first banking - I should have only sat down as I went into the next banking.

Optimum revs never achieved! I knew I could go faster but my legs wouldn't turn the pedals. I'd sat down early for fear of falling off again - I knew not why. Still I rode my heart out - but knew not everything was channelled to my legs. Why? WHY couldn't I gain the speed I knew I was capable of?

It was all over. In floods of tears, I walked away from the track with Andy by my side. 'Well done, Maggie' someone shouted, 'You've clocked 4 minutes 7 seconds!' 'Well, at least I've done a personal best' I thought but ..... would I qualify for the next round?

I didn't qualify from the preliminary rounds. I had ridden my fastest ever pursuit with a time of 4.7.77 but it was not good enough to qualify. I was devastated. Nothing would console me.

That evening, Andy and I sat in the spectator stands watching our GB riders in the team pursuit. As I sat there, I was aware of pigeons in the rafters, flying about. Then it dawned on me .... it must have been a pigeon .... a pigeon had 'pooped' on the track and it was still wet when my wheels touched it .... bringing me down!! The thoughts of what might have been have haunted me for years but at least I know what caused me to fall and it was not my bike handling.

Recovering my composure and being determined to make amends during the World Road Race Championship, the team flew to Cologne.

Understandably very nervous before the start, I had the misfortune to puncture during warming up. Thankfully the tyre was changed and I joined the 60 riders at the start line with a reasonable pace. The route was outside the city and there was one very nasty corner to encounter each of the three laps.

With so many riders (I normally ride in bunches of 40 riders) around me the tension was palpable and needed 100% concentration in order to find and keep my place in the few gaps in the bunch, particularly as the lanes were very narrow. I wanted to get to the front to get in on the 'action' but found it impossible to ride through the bunch, which was literally gutter-to-gutter and no-one would give an inch.

On the second lap I managed to have a short attack on my own but it lasted less than half a mile.

About 3 miles from the finish Anne Reimersma got away but was caught (I thought about trying to jump clear of the bunch up to her but hesitated) and the bunch re-formed.

On the penultimate corner a girl near me crashed, which caused me to swerve near a bollard, and, in doing so I pulled my left foot out of its toe-clip. I had to ease off to replace it and the chase for the finish had already started. Despite my best efforts, I finished 'somewhere' in the main bunch but never did find out what my official position was.

Bette Habetz from West Germany won the race. Brenda Atkinson was the best GB finisher with 9th place.

END OF A DREAM

Chapter 9 – Cycle Racing Results and Photos

Fastest Time Trials

Date	Place	Winner	Second	Third
22 May 1968	Evesham & District Wheelers club event 10 miles	This was my first ever race: 31.08		
19 September 1971	Western TTA event on U11 course 100 miles	Barbara Body 4.32.?	Maggie's time: 4.58.52	
2nd October 1971	Oldbury event on K16 course 25 miles	Gill Clapton Hounslow & District Wheelers 59.04	Maggie's time: 1.1.59	
23 June 1972	Bromsgrove Olympic event on K8 course 10 miles	Christine Goodfellow 23.58	Maggie's time: 24.10	
11 July 1972	National '50' mile on K9 course	Beryl Burton 2.0.33	Maggie's time: 2.14.11	
28 July 1971 **National** **1-hour** **Record** **Attempt**	**Salford Park Track, Birmingham**	**22 miles, 260 yards** **Record never claimed.**		

Team Competition Records gained whilst a member of Beacon Roads Cycling Club:

Date	Event	Distance	Team members	Time
23 June 1972	Bromsgrove Olympic event on K8 course	10 miles	June Pitchford Christine Goodfellow Maggie Gordon Smith	1.13.20
8 July 1972	Stone Wheelers event on J54 course	10 miles	June Pitchford Christine Goodfellow Maggie Gordon Smith	1.12.13

Road Races

Date	Place	Winner	Second	Third
30 May 1971	WCRA Highley, Shropshire	Beryl Burton	First ever road race – didn't know how to race in a bunch	
29 August 1971	Grand Prix Baby Terraneo Mariano Commence, Italy	Morena Tartagni Italy	22nd, nearly last and given a beautiful bronze statue – later given to WCRA (Women's Cycle Racing Association)	
4 September 1971	World Champs, Mendrisio, Switzerland	Anna Konkina Russia	36th. Very hilly course using close ratio block on my borrowed bike	
25 June 1972	National Champs Danebury, Essex	Beryl Burton	14th	
June 1973	3-day stage race – Vlissingen, Holland	Keetie Van Ousten-Hage Holland	22nd overall. WCRA team 8th	
22 July 1973	National Road Race, Yeovil, Somerset	Beryl Burton	10th. Team-mate Christine Goodfellow gained a medal and competed in World Champs.	
July 1974	3-day stage race Le Havre, France.	Beryl Burton	Denise Burton	Jayne Westbury (Maggie 19th)
21 July 1974	National Road Race,	Beryl Burton	Carol Barton	Christine Goodfellow

Date	Place	Winner	Second	Third
	Wakefield, Yorkshire			(Maggie 7th)
29 June 1975	National Road Race, Swindon, Wiltshire	Jayne Westbury	Not sure of other placings – tactical race as Beryl Burton not riding. Maggie 6th	
1976	No racing – got married Now Maggie Thompson			
17 July 1977	National Road Race, Eastway, London	Cathy Swinnerton	Not sure of other placings. Maggie 5th	
3 September 1977	World Road Race San Cristobal, Venezuela	Josianne Bost (France)	Maggie 19th. Did a 'kami-karsi' attack on the penultimate lap and split the field, then got dropped on the last climb.	
23 April 1978	International road race, Dampicourt Belgium	Keetie Van Ousten-Hage	Not sure of other placings. Maggie 21st	
14 May 1978	Hillingdon Ladies & Veterans Road Race	Brenda Atkinson	Maggie Thompson Torrential rain	?
21 July 1978	National Road Race Sutton Bonnington	Brenda Atkinson	Denise Burton	Cathy Swinnerton (Maggie 4th)
6-9 July 1978	3-day stage race Le Havre France	Petra Debruin (Holland)	Pai Prim (Sweden)	**Maggie Thompson (Great Britain) Best ever inter-national performance**

87

Date	Place	Winner	Second	Third
	Queen of the Mountains	Pia Prim (Sweden)	Arlette Lacan (Normandie France)	**Maggie Thompson** **(Great Britain)** **Best ever international performance**
29 July 1978	Keighley Velo Ladies Road Race Skipton, Yorkshire	**Maggie Thompson** **Best ever road race performance**	Josie Heffernan	Brenda Atkinson
24 August 1978	World Road Race, Koln (Cologne), West Germany	Beate Habetz (West Germany)	Maggie??? A competitor crashed in front of me on the penultimate corner causing me to pull my foot out of its pedal just before the final sprint and I finished 'somewhere' in the bunch – no idea of my placing. Very disappointed as had been riding well till that point. Brenda Atkinson 9th.	

3000 metre Ladies National Pursuit results:

Date	Place	Winner	Second	Third
4.8.1971	Kirkby Stadium, Liverpool	Beryl Burton 4.16 minutes	Bernadette Swinnerton 4.22. minutes	Maggie Gordon Smith 4.28 minutes
12.8.1972	Kirkby Stadium, Liverpool	Beryl Burton	Carol Barton	Maggie Gordon Smith 4.36 minutes
3&4.8.1973	Saffron Lane, Leicester	Beryl Burton 4.13 minutes	Carol Barton 4.18 minutes	Maggie Gordon Smith 4.25 minutes
2.8.1974	Saffron Lane, Leicester	Beryl Burton 4.13 minutes	Carol Barton 4.20 minutes	Maggie Gordon Smith 4.21 minutes
30&31.7.1975	Saffron Lane, Leicester	Denise Burton 4.19.1 minutes	Maggie Gordon Smith 4.19.6 minutes	Carol Barton
1976	No racing – got married – now Maggie Thompson			
5.8.1977	Saffron Lane, Leicester	**Maggie Thompson** 4.10 minutes	Denise Burton 4.13 minutes	Beryl Burton
21.7.1978	Saffron Lane, Leicester	**Maggie Thompson** 4.16 minutes	Brenda Atkinson 4.22 minutes	Denise Burton 4.17 minutes

Racing Photos:

Being presented with my first ever medal at the age of 17 by Paul Gittins at the Evesham & District Wheelers prize presentation in 1969.

Trophee Spumador presented to me at Grand Prix Baby Terraneo in 1971 – donated to WCRA – Womens Cycle Racing Assocation.

1975 - Maggie riding to a silver medal in the 3000 metre National Pursuit in Leicester

1977 – Maggie winning the gold medal in the Ladies National Pursuit

1977 – Maggie on the winner's podium for the Ladies National Pursuit flanked by both Denise and Beryl Burton – Leicester

Article in the 1978 National Championship programme –

horrendous photo!!!

Margaret Thompson — Gannett C.C. Ladies 3000 metre Individual Pursuit Champion

When one starts to write about our British 3,000 metres pursuit for la femme, one, I am sure, can be forgiven for automatically writing Burton,Burton, Burton, etc., intermingled with the odd Barton - howbeit that towards the end of some two decades the Beryl Burton, O.B.E. changed to daughter Denise.

This then was the challenge that Margaret Thompson had to face last year. A challenge that dozens and dozens of our girls had had to face for so long, with the general realisation it was a question as to who could come second. Even that position had become somewhat a closed shop with Carol Barton taking that spot on most occasions.

I well remember an extremely quiet and demure Margaret Gordon Smith being

brought onto the tough scene of cycle racing when she was but sweet sixteen. Eventually she reached the bronze medal stage, indeed in our first Newmark series of 1973 and then again in 1974. 1975 brought a final spot against Denise Burton, so she took the silver medal with Carol Barton taking the bronze.

Then came marriage and a year out of the sport and a return to the championships last year. We, in the sport, had longed to bring about a mother-daughter final - we had planned to televise it - but we reckoned without wee Maggie.

In the qualifying round she clocked a good time of 4 mins. 12.43 secs. to Denise's 4 mins. 14.0 secs. and Beryl in fourth place with 4 mins. 22.82 secs. In the quarter-finals the margin narrowed a little. Maggie's time 4.14.35 and Denise 4.15.12. Those of us who had planned for the Burton-Burton final had received a decided slap in the face.

It is history now that celebrated daughter beat world famous mother and that Maggie comfortably beat the attractive Cathy Swinnerton and went on to beat Denise by some 3 seconds - true the positions were later reversed in the World Championships in Venezuela when Denise qualified and was only a second too slow in the quarter-finals and Maggie way below the form she had shown at Leicester failed to qualify.

Recently Denise stopped training. Beryl's tragic early season crash may affect her return to the track, it may spur others to have a go and hopefully to produce a new era of world class women - perhaps Maggie will take a leaf out of Beryl's book.

25

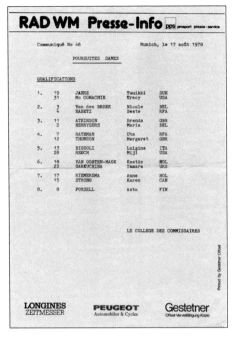

Official communiques for the Ladies World 3000 metre Championships at Munich Olympic velodrome in 1978, showing the preliminary heat I was in on the orange sheet and the times of all the competitors in this heat. I achieved my fastest time over the distance with 4.07.99, slightly slower than that of Brenda Atkinson. There were only two riders slower than me and one didn't finish. At least I knew that taking this race into account I was 12th fastest out of 15 riders at World Championship level and I was 18 seconds slower than Keetie Van Ousten-Hage with her time of 3.49.54.

As of 22 February 2020 Chloe Dygert Owen, a professional racing cyclist from USA broke the world record at the World Championships in Berlin with a time of 3.16.937 on an indoor track.

Maggie with Ladies National Pursuit Champion Trophy – 1977

Maggie with Ladies National
Pursuit Champion Trophy -
1978

Chapter 10 – Lands End to John O'Groats (Stage 2)

17 Home to Wolverhampton Station   Distance: 11 miles

Leaving home for my third stage of LEJOG felt similar to the start of stage 2, knowing that as I left my home mid-morning with my heavily laden bike, I would not return for over a week. Full of anticipation, excitement and a healthy amount of apprehension, I set off through Wordsley and immediately felt the extra weight of full panniers.

Again that strange thought of riding along familiar residential roads through Wall Heath and Swindon to Wombourne – routes I could almost cycle with my eyes closed. Just at the right moment I remembered the disused railway track that I have often cycled and walked along and enjoyed a traffic-free section to Wombourne station where I stopped at the café for my lunch.

I continued my ride along the disused railway track to Castlecroft and then rode into Wolverhampton along quite a busy road through the centre of the city to the railway station. I was early so sat waiting on the platform with my bike, chatting with a lady from Prestatyn who was on her way home after visiting her son and family in London.

My train came in first so I said goodbye to the lady. An impatient porter shouted at me to go to the front carriage where bikes could be stored. His manner was most rude but I got on the train and managed to secure my bike and remove the panniers as the train set off. I found a seat close to my bike so I could keep an eye on it.

I watched the rolling countryside as the train sped past. It wasn't particularly interesting at this point and, with the 'budebumbum' sound of the train, I kept dropping off to sleep until we reached Warrington. The scenery became more interesting and the weather changed from being overcast to having a few sunny spells.

There were several other passengers, either engrossed in books or in their own world wearing earphones. After Preston I knew we would soon be near the Trough of Bowland and looking in the westerly direction I saw the unmistakable outline of the Lake District – views that eluded me last year with poor visibility

I began to get very excited as I recognised the section I had cycled along the Lune valley last year where I could see the M6 and railway line, as the road had climbed towards Shap. I couldn't resist mentioning it to nearby passengers. Soon Penrith and Carlisle appeared and I saw a few relics of snow on Hartside.

The train crossed into Scotland and again sections were familiar to me as it followed my route from last year. I got excited as we reached the Upper Clyde Wind Farm – it looked spectacular and the sun lit up the majestic 'wings' on the turbines. I was entranced.

Soon I recognised a mountain and then realised we were at Lanark – not long to go now. We passed the yellow high-rise flats at Hamilton that I saw last year from miles away and eventually we arrived at Glasgow Central in bright sunshine.

I rode the 2 miles to Kelvingrove and the Youth Hostel, put my bike in the store, got changed and walked out to find somewhere to eat. An Indian Restaurant nearby was recommended called Chillies. My meal promised to be really tasty but the spices were so hot I couldn't taste anything. There was a friendly buzz at the restaurant though.

I walked back to the Youth Hostel and chatted with a lady from Melbourne who flew up from London today. She was planning to take a scenic railway journey tomorrow and stay at Mallaig for a few days.

18 Glasgow to Stirling   Distance: 35.5 miles

I chatted with the other ladies in my dormitory this morning then fetched my bike and enjoyed a leisurely ride though Kelvingrove Park. Memories flooded back from my visit last year when the park was filled with people sunbathing whilst enjoying a heat wave – not so today.

Soon I found my road to Kelvinsdale and gingerly descended a steep hill (14%) as the entrance to the Forth & Clyde canal was at the bottom and I joined its towpath heading east. The canal was wider than those local to my home with equally wider towpaths. Along the whole towpath section the surface ranged from muddy and rutted to smooth, gravelly tarmac. I hadn't been on the towpath long when it went up a sequence of about 5 staircase locks, about the size of Caen locks in Wiltshire.

It must have been around the Stockingfield Junction that I followed the path to the right by a block of flats that led me to the city centre ….. and off-course! Thinking back, I couldn't recall the opportunity to change my route earlier but, if I hadn't taken the wrong route I would not have passed Partick Thistle's football ground or reached a viewpoint where I could almost see the Youth Hostel and the university.

I ended up near Port Dundes and rode on to a main road to re-join the canal by Larkhill. Getting back on the canal towpath again was like being in another world with no motor traffic, much greenery, birdsong and seeing the water lily leaves nearly reaching the surface of the canal. Some sections alongside the canal looked quite marshy and I could just make out some mountains to my left through the poor visibility. There weren't that many other people on the towpath other than a group of cyclists on a fundraising bike ride for disadvantaged children from Larkhill.

I soon found myself passing sites of Roman forts as I approached Kirkintilloch. The map on my Garmin Satnav showed that I was very near to the site of the Roman Antonine Wall.

I came across a runner who I passed and we played 'catch' for some distance as I stopped to take photos until he turned around to retrace – he was running at quite a pace.

Soon I began to feel rain and by the time I reached Kilsyth, I was very wet – I put overshoes on and, whilst bending down, got a soaking on my backside! Feeling very soggy I got back on my bike and continued on the towpath until I reached Banknock where I left the canal and headed north on a little lane that went seriously uphill! Whilst riding up this hill I heard a rumble of thunder, which left me feeling quite nervous and vulnerable.

Aware that I was getting quite hungry, I stopped by a tree despite the torrential rain and thunder and ate my sandwich. I could hear a motorway or busy road nearby and was aware that if I turned right I would cross it so I could join a main road leading to Denny. I rode through this town's by-pass and took the road that ran alongside the motorway, completely ignoring my planned route through lanes as all I cared about was reaching the Youth Hostel in Stirling and getting out of my soaking clothes.

It was with great disappointment that I passed the heritage centre at Bannockburn – it was the reason I had given myself a short ride today so that I could visit it. However, I had to be sensible – I could end up with a chill if I hung around in wet clothes. I was just about maintaining my body warmth as it was by continuing to ride.

I phoned the Youth Hostel to ask if I could arrive early. It was 1.30 pm and was so thankful when they said they would be open at 2.00 pm. I carried on towards Stirling Castle and up a long steep hill leading up to the Hostel.

Despite dripping everywhere as I went inside the Hostel, I was made to feel very welcome. I took my stuff to the dormitory and had stripped off about to have a shower when I remembered that I'd left my bike outside the main entrance. Thankfully, the lady on duty had put it away for me. The shower was bliss and I soon warmed up.

I was grateful to be able to make use of a washing and drying machine.

Later in the afternoon it stopped raining and wasn't cold so I was able to venture outside again and explore the city. I was fascinated to find so many historic buildings linked to major people in Scotland's history.

Walking to the top of the hill to the castle I found I was too late to visit it and enjoyed fantastic views from the walls by the entrance. There was a statue to King Robert the Bruce and to the east was a hill with a huge monument to William Wallace! It was in a most dramatic setting.

Returning to the Hostel I decided to have my supper there rather than go out again. The chef was very friendly and I managed to sneak in the dining hall before a large group of students arrived.

Back in my dormitory, I had a thorough look at my route for the next day and chatted to Jenny, my roommate. She was staying here whilst doing a weekend semester for her course to become a swimming teacher.

19 Stirling to Crianlarich   Distance: 54.5 miles

I woke quite early and was glad to see it wasn't raining other than 'Scotch Mist' from the very low clouds.

Loading my bike and setting off, I soon got myself on the main road towards Callender. The road was pretty straight and flat but busy and thankfully I seemed to have a tailwind so flew along at around 14 mph.

It was strange riding along knowing there were mountains around me but I could only see a little way up and the rest was a total mystery in the mist.

I had a couple of false starts at Callender and eventually found the National Cycle Route 7, which was immediately delightful. I hadn't realised how much the constant traffic noise had been getting to me and now I could hear the birds singing and lambs bleating in the fields. The disused railway line that was NCN 7 was wonderfully peaceful and the surface was very good. Several times I came across walkers and other cyclists but on the whole I had it to myself.

Soon after joining the route I could hear rushing water and this turned out to be the Falls of Deny as the river from Loch Lubnaig passed through a woody gorge. Soon the route opened out revealing low hanging clouds that were beginning to lift and reveal the mystery of the surrounding mountains.

I wasn't far from Strathyre when the track split and I found myself descending towards the loch. On reflection, perhaps I should have taken the track leading uphill as it was wider and possibly better defined. However, I followed the arrow signposts despite my Garmin GPS showing that I was riding along 'thin air' as the track wasn't marked and I was clearly 'off course'. I soon found myself on a 'Lombard Street' like climb (San Francisco) and had to walk a short distance, as I hadn't anticipated needing my inner chain ring to access my lowest gear!

Soon I was on a better route having re-joined the correct one and reached the sign to Strathyre. I was on the point of leaving NCN 7 to re-join the main road but checked my map and found that if I stayed on it I could reach Balquhidder where Rob Roy was buried. The route was rewarding with lovely switchbacks through trees and the occasional house. On turning into the village I was treated to a lovely view of Loch Voil – again with the clouds lifting further. Luckily, when I found the church, two men were taking photos and pointed out the grave of Rob Roy to me – I never realised he lived until   he   was   63! (https://en.wikipedia.org/wiki/Rob_Roy_MacGregor)

I continued along the A85 at Balquhidder Station, taking the road to Lochearnhead. Then came the climb up Glen Ogle. It was a long drag but I didn't need my lowest gears. The clouds were lifting further and the River Ogle gurgled first on my left and then the road crossed it so it was on my right. The traffic was pretty heavy – a lot of motorcyclists out for the day and some obviously touring. As I puffed and panted on my way up, I noticed route NCN 7 on my left up higher up the mountain. It went over an impressive viaduct in stunning scenery and I wished I could have ridden along it, but it was going away from my planned route.

Near the top of the climb I looked down into the pasture and saw a lone lamb – we had eye contact and all of a sudden, it started bounding up towards me up a steep incline bleating like mad. I couldn't see any other sheep or lambs nearby and couldn't help but feel it was a cry for help to find it's mother. I felt awful just carrying on but there was nothing I could do for it. If I had stopped maybe it would have been too frightened and run off again. That haunted me for some time to come.

The descent was fantastic and my speed went up to 39 mph – so exhilarating! It was now mid-afternoon and I only had another 11 miles to do to my destination for the day, so I took a 2 ½ mile detour to the village of Killin, enjoying more of a descent (knowing I would have to climb back up again). The River Dochart descends into Killin and by the centre of the village it becomes bubbling rapids – the Falls of Dochart. There were loads of people enjoying this spectacular sight, even people paddling in the safe shallows. I also noticed a sign to the burial ground of the Clan Macnab right beside the river – see: http://clan-macnab.com/inchbuie-or-innes-bhuidhe-the-yellow-island-the-ancient-burial-ground-of-clan-macnab/.

I climbed back up the hill to continue my route, noticing that the clouds had almost gone in places and I could see the tops of the Moainsunt. Some mountains still shrouded in light clouds gave me glimpses of where they still had some patches of snow and let my imagination run wild trying to see more of the mountain that was still hidden.

The road was very busy with traffic and gently undulating but I became aware of a slight westerly wind against me. The worst part of the final miles was the road surface. It was bumpier than any of NCN 7 with large pieces of stone in the tarmac that sent vibrations up my arms – not to mention the sore nether regions of my backside!

I passed Loch Dochart and began to think I would never reach Crianlarich when all of a sudden I saw the sign to my B&B. It was late afternoon when I arrived and I was grateful to be able to 'stop' and freshen up. After struggling to get a wi-fi signal at the B&B I did manage to send a text to Steve before going to the Benmore Lodge for my evening meal.

20 Crianlarich to Glencoe   Distance: 39 miles

I joined the other guests at breakfast and found a couple and another man had frightening experiences whilst walking yesterday; they became disorientated by the low cloud. The couple managed to find their way down the mountain they climbed and the other man nearly completed a major climb but concluded the conditions were too dangerous to continue. I felt lucky that cycling mostly along main roads on this section ensured I wouldn't become lost.

The road to Tyndrum wasn't too busy and although it was overcast, it showed no sign of rain. I set off on the A82 towards Glencoe. The road turned sharp right and immediately I had to use my inner chain-ring to climb a long hill. Thankfully, it soon evened out and I kept a good pace with little or no wind. As I climbed, I could clearly see the bottom of the mountains surrounding me; the rest was shrouded in mist, which as it began to lift, left my mind tantalised as I tried to imagine what lay out of sight.

I then enjoyed a long descent to the Bridge of Orchy (feeling sorry for another touring cyclist slogging his way up in the opposite direction). I soon came across the edge of Loch Tulla with mountains at its edge, which was still as a millpond with perfect reflections. A long hard climb followed – there was practically a hairpin bend at the bottom. The traffic was very heavy and, at one point, I felt very vulnerable as a 'convoy' of traffic came past me including several coaches. These were far too close together and quite plainly didn't have a chance to see me – they passed so close leaving me very little room. It was the scariest part of my ride so far as I had the choice of being squashed or falling at the side of a long, steep bank if they hit me.

There was a viewpoint half-way up the climb and I stopped to gather my wits and admire the view. A piper in kilt and tartan stood with an atmospheric view behind him and played for the many tourists wandering about the viewpoint. I also took the opportunity to plead with a couple of coach drivers to allow a bit more room and space between vehicles in order to consider cyclists.

After a bit more climbing my excitement grew as I entered Rannoch Moor with its many scattered small lochs. This Moor is renowned for its eerie atmosphere in certain weather conditions but today it felt gentle and serene. Whilst riding this section I was overjoyed to hear not one but two cuckoos! What I wasn't expecting was how high the mountains were that surrounded it. Several still had quite a lot of snow on them. Soon I reached the point where Rannoch Moor and Glencoe merged and I can't describe how elated I felt. I had the most perfect weather – still a few wisps of cloud on the mountains but … there was sunshine too; it just got better and better. I didn't want to blink my eyes – the sight before me was just so awesome!

The 8-miles to reach the bottom at Glencoe took me 1½ hours! My senses were on overload, I couldn't get enough of my surroundings and kept stopping to take photographs, videos or just to stop and drink in this once in a lifetime experience on my bike

It seemed Glencoe has its own weather conditions and I had quite a strong headwind to contend with. Also, my mind was playing tricks on me as I thought I should be descending to Glencoe but my legs were telling me a different story – the mountains certainly looked taller the further ahead they were. Often on my mind was concern about what the weather conditions would be like a couple of days ahead, on my way to Altnahara – a very remote and exposed section of my route.

I rode through the Pass of Glencoe, which was hemmed in by rocky cliffs on both sides. This gorge was around 1 mile long and although it seemed shorter than Cheddar Gorge it was utterly spectacular! Almost immediately afterwards I took the opportunity to stop and have my picnic. To my right was the babbling and chuckling stream of the River Coe – a more perfect picnic site I cannot imagine. I could hardly tear myself away.

A short distance ahead I reached a parking place with an information board about the Three Sisters Mountains that are a classic landmark of Glencoe and again stopped to simply drink in the splendour of what I saw. Not much further to go and I took a lane to the right to find the Youth Hostel along a quiet lane, away from all the traffic.

It was a glorious afternoon and, as I'd arrived early, I asked to drop off my entire luggage in my dormitory so I could go and explore the village of Glencoe. I had quite a long descent through the leafy lane and found a café. Across the road was a long low cottage painted white with a thatch. This was the Folklore Museum and fascinating to look around to learn about the life of the locals in years gone by. Displayed in a glass cabinet were several pieces of Mauchline Ware, which I was delighted to see and told the custodian of my family's link to these collectable decorative wooden boxes. Ancestors of my father lived in Mauchline in Ayrshire – William and Andrew Smith – and set up a business creating these boxes. There is a collectors society for these boxes: http://mauchlineware.com/index.php . I recall a story my father told as he attended one of their conventions. The speaker was making the point that there were no more living relatives; to which my father piped up that he was a direct descendent. After providing more information about his ancestral heritage, the society was pleased to accept his family tie to the business.

I was saddened to learn about the 'Massacre of Glencoe' in 1692. The Clan Macdonald didn't swear allegiance to King William and Mary by the appointed time so the whole family was massacred! This eventually led to the Jacobite Rebellions. (https://www.visitscotland.com/about/history/jacobites/)

I rode back to the Hostel and it was great to meet Gill who shared my dormitory. She comes from Edinburgh and climbed one of the munro's (mountains over 3000 feet) of Glencoe today – on her own!! She was doing a mountain leadership course and this was part of her training. She's really enjoying the course as it is making her aware of the flora and fauna she encounters giving her an all-round experience to pass on to people she will be leading. Gill also delivers Reiki and could relate to Laughter Yoga when I explained it to her. Later we met Kay who is also sharing our dormitory and comes from Brecon. Kay was also doing walks on her own and had been travelling the West Highland Way, which I had seen several times today. I felt very inspired by these two ladies and wouldn't have the confidence to be completely on my own on the mountains in such a remote area, particularly with the recent weather conditions.

I walked to the Clachaig Inn – a well-known mountaineering 'watering hole' that is now a posh restaurant. Here in the rustic bar I ate a delicious venison stew and enjoyed the walk back to the hostel still listening to the calls of cuckoos.

21 Glencoe to Fort Augustus   Distance: 51 miles

After having breakfast with Gill and Kay I set off in good weather - bright and sunny but cold. I was able to ride along the shared use path to Ballachulish and then crossed the bridge to North Ballachulish. I could smell the sea, as this was a sea loch going up to Fort William.

From here I had to ride on the A82, which was very busy with traffic. There were some very posh houses on the way to Fort William and I stopped to have a look around the shops. I found Alpine Bikes and asked them to adjust my brakes and put some more air in my back tyre.

I got on my bike and almost immediately felt something was wrong – there was a regular 'bump, bump, bump' on my back wheel. On investigation, I could see that the tyre had not bedded into the rim by the valve. I let out some air and walked back to Alpine Bikes. After several attempts to put the tyre back inside the rim it was clear that the beading on the tyre had worn out and they fitted a new tyre for me. I was so grateful this problem happened within easy access of a bike shop.

Soon I was back on the road towards Corpach where I got on to the Caledonian Canal at Neptune's Staircase – a large set of staircase locks making Nine Locks near home at Brierley Hill look quite insignificant.

It was wonderful to be off the A82 and soon I found I had the best view of Ben Nevis I had ever seen. The towpath was pretty good and I had a tailwind! The canal was very wide but not as wide as the River Severn. I stopped at one point to try my iPhone and found that at last I had a signal so sent emails to my family – then it died on me!

As I rode along the canal towpath, the sweet scent of Broom filled my nostrils – like a combination of vanilla and pineapple.

Occasionally there were some boats but not like the narrowboats I am used to seeing in the Black Country, more like ocean-going yachts.

I came across a couple with their dogs – the lady was walking and the man was on a recumbent tricycle. As we chatted, I learned that the man had a suffered a major Stroke 12 years ago, losing, speech and mobility. Over the intervening years he had recovered much of it and could speak coherently now but his mobility is still poor and he couldn't use his right arm and hand at all. The recumbent has been a godsend for them so that they can both still enjoy getting out and about in the fresh air and all the controls are operated by his left hand. I felt quite humbled and inspired by this couple.

I carried on to Gairlochy to have my picnic lunch and was delighted to find this lock had a swing bridge. Barriers were put up by the lockmaster to stop cars going over whilst 2 large boats went through. I took a video of the swing bridge in operation knowing that my partner, Steve would be fascinated by it: https://canmore.org.uk/site/159077/caledonian-canal-gairlochy-swing-bridge

Having spoken to a couple of walkers at the lock, I decided to make use of the Great Glen Way so that I could keep off the A82 and set off along a delightful hilly lane to Clunes. From here I was able to join the Great Glen Way along a wide and well-surfaced forestry path. This was a delightful track with wide and open views across Loch Lochy and I could still see the Ben Nevis range

The track stopped at South Laggan and I managed to get back on to the Caledonian Canal to North Laggan and then was forced back onto the A82 again for a short period. I passed through Invergarry and on to the Bridge of Oich. From here I was able to re-join the Caledonian Canal for the final section to Fort Augustus. It had been a long day but very pleasant with a large section of it off-road.

There was another impressive lock flight at Fort Augustus and then a killer of a climb to reach Morag's Lodge – an independent Youth Hostel. Modern and comfortable with a very laid-back atmosphere. My roommate was Shirley with a South African accent. She does some physiotherapy and was interested in Laughter Yoga. She came up to Fort Augustus to attend an interview with the Forestry Commission and was now taking a break.

I went to have my evening meal at the Hostel and a huge party arrived. The huge lasagne cooked at the Hostel was absolutely delicious and one of the best meals of my tour. I sat with 3 much-travelled ladies who were on a 'Haggis Adventure' coach trip. One lady in particular had been all over the world and another is planning a world tour. They started talking about shopping and I felt out of my depth, as that is not my 'thing'. However, they were interested in my cycling holiday.

Afterwards Shirley and I joined everyone else in the bar. We had a great evening. The Haggis Adventure coach trip group were doing a Karaoke and, just for once, I joined in and found it a great laugh. There was such a great atmosphere there with everyone letting go and enjoying themselves. Shirley was great company too along with 2 other friends, one of whom had been at the same interview as Shirley today and she'd given him a lift to it. We turned in just before 11 pm – a late night but great fun.

22 Fort Augustus to Culbokie   Distance: 42 miles

Woke to a lovely bright morning and chatted with Shirley as we sat outside eating our breakfast. I really enjoyed Shirley's company – we clicked straight away and I felt we were kindred spirits. I mentioned my friend Jules Mitchell's mantra of 'SIT' (Surprised, Inspired and Touched) and actually feel Shirley has both inspired and touched me.

I set off and found myself back on the A82 towards Inverness with Loch Ness on my right. The ride was quite easy with a tailwind and bright sunshine. I stopped 4 miles out of Fort Augustus at a layby right next to the loch and went to have a closer look where I saw a breath-taking view of the loch - a deep shade of blue surrounded by mountains. Soon I arrived at Invermorriston and stopped to admire an ancient bridge built practically into cliffs.

I reached Castle Urquhart and took the opportunity to visit this historic landmark and stronghold. King Edward I took it during the 13th century and Robert the Bruce took it back in 1308. The Grant family owned it for some time and the Macdonalds, who considered themselves almost the Scottish Monarchy, fought a massive battle there and took possession of it – that might have led to the Massacre of Glencoe! See: https://en.wikipedia.org/wiki/Urquhart_Castle

The castle was extremely busy with sightseers arriving by the coachload. The man at the pay desk took one look at my 'Get Cycling' tabard and asked me if I was on a sponsored ride. When I answered 'yes' he allowed me in for free so I put the £6.40 entrance fee in the sponsorship 'kitty'. I had a look around for about an hour, dodging squally showers before continuing my ride to Milton. Another squally shower and I took refuge under the open canopy of a garage to someone's house, hoping they didn't mind me taking advantage of the shelter it offered. Resuming my ride, I took a right turn along a quieter road that climbed quite steeply towards Beauly. I nearly managed to ride it all but was beaten by a section of 15% incline so walked about 80 metres. It was very remote at the top, reminiscent of Rannoch Moor in places.

On approaching an interesting descent with a sweeping double bend on a quiet lane, I thought it would make an interesting video on the way down. Warning myself not to go too fast, I set off very gingerly with my camcorder in my right hand whilst I controlled the bike with my left hand. It did occur to me that this was rather a foolhardy activity (and most likely illegal) but I ignored my inner warnings and continued, feeling pleased with my stunning clip. I was so engrossed looking at the picture on the camcorder screen that I failed to notice I was heading straight for a very nasty pothole and I went flying! A bit shaken, I picked myself off the floor and was in the process of picking up my bike when a truck came hurtling down the hill and screeched to a halt. The driver and passenger quickly came to my aid and checked me over. They brought out first aid and cleaned the grazes I had on my fingers. I felt so embarrassed and stupid but they were very kind and they watched me pedal off to make sure I was OK. I was SO cross with myself for being so stupid!

I continued riding down Glen Convinth, enjoying the lovely scenery. I stopped to attend to a minor mishap on my bike following my fall and could hear the sound of bagpipes. The only conclusion I could come up with was that someone at the farm nearby was practising – it sounded haunting and completely authentic.

Soon I arrived at Beauly, an interesting small town with an unusual Priory of the Valliscaulians Order from France – I'd never heard of them before: https://en.wikipedia.org/wiki/Beauly_Priory . I ate my lunch in the town square and chatted to two local lads. I also called at the hotel hoping they could give me the contact for the local paper, as I wanted to write a letter of thanks to my two 'knights' that helped me when I came off my bike.

I continued my ride towards Muir of Ord, dodging heavy showers and struggling against a strengthening wind.

Now I was out of large mountains to a more gently undulating area but the lanes were still quite hilly and there was quite a strong cross-wind. These made the last 7 miles quite difficult, as I felt exposed to the wind. With around 2 miles left to reach Culbokie – my destination for today, I had been watching an approaching storm for several minutes. I came across a lady in her garden with a lovely ornamental telephone box in her garden. I asked to take shelter and she told me to make the most of her spacious garage, I was most grateful as I would indeed have got a soaking had I tried to continue.

Finally, I reached Netherton Farm at Culbokie and was relieved to have stayed dry. I was shown my room, which looked straight over Cromarty Firth. Watching the weather forecast on the TV I became very concerned about my ride tomorrow to Altnahara and even considered riding to Inverness and 'calling it a day' for this stage of my ride. The forecast was for gale-force winds coming down from the north. I was planning to head north, straight into the path of these gales and Altnahara is an exposed and very remote area.

23 Culbokie to Brora   Distance: 49 miles

It was with a sense of trepidation that I woke this morning. Concerned what to do after yesterday's very strong winds and the forecast for today of more gale force winds. Reluctantly, I decided not to go to Altnahara – I'd been really looking forward to going, partly in the excitement of going somewhere so remote and partly in fear and awe of such remoteness.

I picked up my iPhone and found a morale-boosting message from Steve, telling me not to give up when I was so close to my goal and to consider riding the A9 all along the east coast. After my despondency, his words were full of encouragement and I wished I could have hugged him there and then!

I shared my breakfast with one other guest – a man who regularly stays there who works on the oil rigs nearby. It was good to chat to my landlady after breakfast, as we didn't get a chance yesterday whilst she was giving some Spanish lessons. She was most helpful and we tried to make contact with various Tourist Information Offices along my newly planned route to secure accommodation for this evening. Eventually, she suggested I try a Tourist Office in Tain, which would be the first big town I would reach.

The wind wasn't too bad this morning as I set off down the hill from Netherton Farm to meet the A9. I turned right and immediately began to cross the long bridge over Cromarty Firth. There was a footpath so I rode on that to keep out of the traffic. I found a quieter road to Evanton and bought a road map from a petrol station. At Alness I returned to the A9 and continued the 20 miles to reach Tain – at one point passing an oil rig in Cromarty Firth. It rained heavily on and off with a northerly wind but the terrain was fairly flat with large mountains further inland. The road turned northwards and I hit the headwind and rain again as I reached Tain. I couldn't see a Tourist Office but went into some municipal buildings where I was told Tain didn't have one and they suggested I try Dornoch, which was about 10 miles away.

Just after Tain the sun came out for a short while as I passed the Glenmorangie Whisky Distillery. I then had to cross Dornoch Firth – straight into the strengthening northerly wind. At 5 mph I felt I was riding too slowly to be safe so dismounted and walked across. There was a small 'barrage' at the end, but I could hardly hear its turbines because of the howling wind. I then had to climb up 'The Mound' and shortly afterwards turned right (with a tailwind at last) to Dornoch.

What a delightful place – a real surprise with Royal connections in its past. With a stately mansion in local stone, it was rather like Broadway in its magnificence.

I called at the Tourist Office and the ladies found me a B&B just outside Brora, which was 17 miles away but there was no answer from their phone. I was not keen to ride on and call on them on the off chance that they would be able to accommodate me. As it happened, another lady was in the office, herself a visitor from Atlanta, Georgia and she approached me to make an amazing offer, not sure whether it was the right thing to do. She had hired a cottage in Brora for her holiday and offered for me to stay with her as she had plenty of spare room. This was how I met Sally Hudson Ross and I was extremely grateful to her! She had things to do in Dornoch and wouldn't get there until late afternoon. With time to spare, I spent a good hour looking around Dornoch before setting off for Brora.

Dornoch Castle is now a hotel and the parish church is a 'cathedral' – where, incidentally, Madonna 'secretly' married Guy Richie. The small museum revealed a lot about life in the town and also about the Meikle ferry disaster on 16 August 1809, when ninety-nine people perished when the ferry was overloaded and met a heavy swell in the Dornoch Firth and sank: https://en.wikipedia.org/wiki/Meikle_Ferry_disaster. The Cathedral had also suffered from various fires caused by battles between the Clans.

Reluctant to leave delightful Dornoch, I set off again, enjoying the delightful lane out of the town, passing Embo and along Loch Fleet … into the full force of the North wind and frequent showers. I passed Skelbo castle ruin and enjoyed the views across the Loch towards Littleferry and Golspie. I could hardly hold my camera steady whilst trying to take photos as bushes of Broome were being jostled by the wind, which was howling eerily.

The wind was strengthening and I could do no more than 6 mph as I reached a bridge and struggled over it. I then changed direction and had a fantastic tailwind that enabled me to 'fly' to Golspie at 16 mph!

Unfortunately, as I had to re-join the A9, the ride to Brora afterwards meant that I changed direction again with tremendous frightening gusts from my left side, throwing me into the main road towards busy traffic. I had to lean heavily to my left constantly, didn't dare to get out of the saddle or take my hands off my handlebars to wipe the rain dripping from my streaming nose. I was not a pretty sight and my hands and backside felt numb. It really was the most frightening weather conditions I have ever cycled in.

Just as I reached Brora, I stopped to allow a lorry pass me and who should be behind it but Sally so I followed her through Brora and she kept stopping for me at strategic junctions. We turned left at a petrol station heading towards the Clynelish distillery. The lane to her cottage was longer than I expected and straight into the gale-force winds. I was glad she kept stopping for me, as I don't think I would have found her cottage otherwise.

On reaching her cottage, we brought everything inside, including my bike and it took the full weight of both of us to close her front door, as the wind was so strong. The sound of the wind roared around the cottage and the top of the ventilator over the kitchen kept banging.

I was so grateful to Sally for her hospitality. After a relaxing bath and change of clothes, we chatted for some time and felt very comfortable in each other's company. Her husband, Rex, passed away in 2010 and they had done a lot of travelling together. He had a lung bypass that gave them five more years together before he passed away from bladder cancer. They often visited this part of Scotland and she knows a lot of people at Dornoch where she has stayed before. She's at Brora this time as it is close to a golf course and she competes successfully, despite a bad knee.

Later, once the winds had settled down, she drove me to her golf club overlooking the sea and we had a drink whilst enjoying a succession of rainbows over the sea – we both dashed outside with our cameras to take photos. Then, after a little drive around Brora, we went to Brora Bistro, a restaurant Sally wanted to try out.

After the meal we had a short drive to a small loch to enjoy the fading light before returning and watching some TV together.

We enjoyed a smashing evening chatting like two long lost friends. Sally planned to do a short cruise around southern Norway and also to visit Amsterdam before going home. She has two sisters who don't live close by in the US but keep in regular contact. Sally was a professor of English literature and studied at Exeter, UK. She and Rex also visited the Lake District, particularly for Wordsworth and fell in love with the region, particularly whilst staying at Ullswater.

114

I had a lovely breakfast with Sally and gave her a taster of Laughter Yoga. Not sure whether she felt comfortable, but I know she enjoyed the relaxation at the end. Sally provided me with a packed lunch and it was with great reluctance that I left her to ride to Thurso riding down hill and passing the old Clynelish distillery to re-join the A9. She had really been my angel at my time of need.

What a different day today – hardly any wind and lovely sunshine, I was almost too hot. I stopped at a cafe at Helmsdale and the lady warned me about a very steep hill at Berridale Brae between 8 – 10 miles away.

My speed was sometimes only 6 mph and others around 14 mph, depending on the terrain – I had a long hill to climb out of Helmsdale. The sea views were stunning, particularly with the Broome so I periodically stopped to take photos and videos.

Soon a cyclist who was also riding LEJOG in 11 days caught me up and I rode with him for a few miles. I stopped to take a photo and his two teammates caught me up just as we reached the descent of Berridale Brae - the hill the lady at the café warned me about. I shouted a warning to the two cyclists and rode down the 13% winding descent very gingerly and started the winding climb – also 13%. About 3 mph was the best I could do.

Eventually, I reached the top and was rewarded with breath-taking views along the coast. The road undulated for several miles as I rode towards Latheronwheel. I came across the prettiest cottage I have seen along the whole journey called Toremore. It was painted white and, on the wall facing the road, a hedge was cut in the shape of a huge heart – a splendid example of topiary and really lived up to being 'home is where the heart is'. I later discovered it was actually a B&B.

At Latheron there were superb sea views with rocky stacks

and then the A9 and my route to Thurso turned left inland. I now had 23 more miles to reach Thurso and the scenery changed dramatically, becoming bare, remote with peat bogs on either side that stretched for miles. I felt quite intimidated and vulnerable as I stopped to eat my picnic and was glad of the odd passing car to relieve how lonely it felt. The weather was in my favour being bright with perfect visibility – I bet it would have felt very sinister in wet or foggy conditions, especially in yesterday's conditions!

At one point I looked back the way I'd come and saw mountains inland that I couldn't see from the coast road – there is a good chance they were around Lairg where I would have gone on my way to Altnahara. One or two of these mountains reminded me of the 'Chain des Volcans' and Puy de Dome in particular in France, as they looked so conical. As I took in the whole view, I saw quite a large Wind Farm ahead of me – it took around 10 miles to reach it. There were 16 Turbines at Causewaymire Wind Farm near Halsary.

Soon pine forests replaced the peat bogs, which I thought was a shame as they were destroying centuries of natural heritage. I passed Halkirk and saw a sign stating 6 miles left to reach Thurso – and I could see the town in the distance. There seemed to be some hills beyond it too, which I found confusing as Thurso is on the north coast!

At last I arrived in Thurso and went straight to a café. The ladies gave me directions where I could reach the beach. What a treat was in store for me. I could see Dunnet Head to my right and straight in front of me were the Orkney Islands – they were so clear I felt I could nearly touch them and yet they were quite a few miles away. The view also explained the mountains I could see earlier that were beyond Thurso. I chatted to some other visitors who told me that today was the first time they had been able to see the Orkneys all week as it had been too misty and they also pointed out 'The Old Man of Hoy'!

I went on to Sandra's Backpacker's Hostel and was able to

take my bike into the Common Room. I only had to pay £14.40 for the night and that included breakfast! It was very basic and I was glad to have a dormitory to myself so I could choose which of the 3 beds I would sleep in – one of them had such a worn out mattress that it sank in the middle. I phoned Steve and left a message for Sally too. I came back to the Hostel after going out for my supper. A young couple were looking on You Tube and I suggested they look at the Skype Laughter Chain featuring a famous man in Laughter Yoga circles called Doug Collins from Mississippi who laughs by saying 'heauw,   heauw': (https://www.youtube.com/watch?v=p32OC97aNqc), – they were in stitches and then they showed me one called 'Dad at Comedy Store', which featured Doug again– it was hilarious.

25 – Thurso to Wick via John O Groats   Distance 22 miles

Having woken early I decided to get a really early start. I called at the bakery for a sandwich and to have my LEJOG record signed and set off on a bright sunny morning.

I missed my turning onto a lane initially but it enabled me to take a photo of a 'Folly' just outside Thurso, near to the ruined castle. I then found my lane along NCN Route 1, which climbed out of the town quite a long way revealing superb views across to the Orkneys and Dunnet Head.

It was a glorious morning; almost warm enough for short sleeves. The lane was so quiet too, a real treat. Soon I turned left along a lovely switchback lane that led me back to the main road at Castletown. Then I rode to Dunnet Bay and could clearly see the rock strata of the cliffs. Unfortunately, I didn't feel I could risk taking time out to ride the 5 miles or so to the end of Dunnet Head as I needed to be at Wick for 4.00 pm to catch my train to Inverness.

I was now getting really excited as the end of my adventure was nearly here – I was no more than 8 miles away. It was a strange feeling of mixed emotions as my mind switched from elation for my achievement to sadness that my adventure was coming to an end. I saw several other cyclists coming from John O'Groats and we made excited exchanges with each other. I presumed they were just starting the 'JOGLE' – end-to-end the other way around.

Soon I became aware of another island, closer than the Orkneys – this was Stroma. Over 300 people had inhabited it in its heyday but the last family left in 1964 and their houses could still be seen clearly dotted all over the island.

It was 10.45 am when I made my final left turn at John O'Groats to reach the 'First and Last House' and the tourist complex right by the sea cliffs. There was a posh hotel there and café's, craft shops and memorabilia. A photographer had set himself by 'the signpost' and I paid £10 to have my 'official' photograph taken – he even added a signpost from Stourbridge stating 585 miles (as the crow flies) as the distance covered from home. He took a couple of photos and also one using my camera and will post the 'official' one to me. I then visited the 'First and Last House' to have my LEJOG record signed for the last time to complete it.

As I left the shop I met a couple in the car park who'd arrived in a campervan and were accompanying two cyclists in their 60's who were about to arrive. They'd passed me several times on my ride and I remember their campervan passing me along the road beside Loch Ness as they had a big sponsorship poster in the back window.

To complete the northern-eastern end of my adventure, I set off to ride the last 2 miles to the lighthouse at Duncansby Head. After a steady climb, I turned a corner and had an exhilarating descent followed by a steep winding ascent, needing bottom gear, along this roller-coaster lane. The ride was well worth it with panoramic views of Dunnet Head, along the length of view of the Orkneys to an outreach lighthouse and finally the Duncansby Head lighthouse. There were several other people there, looking at the views through telescopes – again, the visibility was perfectly clear – I was so lucky. As I retraced my route back to John O'Groats, a view along the coast caught my eye. I left my bike at the side of the lane and walked across the land and there I had a fantastic view of the Duncansby Stacks – they almost looked volcanic and very jagged.

I would have loved to stay an extra day so that I could have taken a trip to Orkney – I would love to see the archaeological site of Scara Brae.

LEJOG Final train ride home   Distance: 9.5 miles

My trip was not yet over however as I needed to ride on to Wick

There was a long steady climb out of John O'Groats but the views were fantastic. It was warm and sunny and I seemed to have a tailwind – I felt as though I was flying, particularly on the long descents.

Soon I reached Keiff, a small fishing village around 8 miles from Wick. Feeling hungry (it was now around 2 pm), I turned left into the village following the promising sign towards the harbour to eat my sandwich. As I rode down past a row of houses, I was aware that something was 'going on', as there was a party of motorcyclists on Harley Davidsons outside one of the houses. Apparently, they were the escort for a bride who was about to come out of one of the houses. Intrigued, I decided to wait – with camera and video at the ready. Around 10 minutes later the bridesmaids emerged and then out she came with her father. She wore a white shift dress, ruffled to one side making that side look like a fan and she had long dark hair. I took photos and videos and promised one of the guests that I would send them on. The bride got into a car and around 12 Harley

Davidsons escorted the whole entourage. What a surprise encounter. Later, I met a man in his garden and managed to get the gist of the address for the couple so I could send on my photos.

I reached Wick around 30-minutes later and to my utter amazement, the whole wedding party were gathered outside a church as I rode into the town! I took a few more photos, as they all got ready to drive off to their reception and then carried on to find the station. (Once I was home I sent the photos and video on a CD and had a lovely 'thank you' letter from the couple after they returned from their honeymoon.)

At the station I sat in the sun whilst waiting for the 2-coach train to be ready to board for Inverness. There was a party of 6 ladies in my carriage having a whale of a time. It turned out they were old school friends going for a meal at Brora Bistro so I was able to tell them how nice it was. They were laughing their heads off and one felt a little guilty leaving me out of their hilarity, so I joined in and did a bit of Laughter Yoga with them too.

The train went to Georgemas Junction first and then Thurso and then back Georgemas before heading in a more southerly direction. At one point, beside a small river, I looked out of the window to see 2 young lads with their backs to the train drop their trousers and 'mooned' at us. I was in hysterics!

The train was faster than our 'trundler' from Stourbridge but as was evident from the state of my notes, it was very bumpy – a real 'boody-bum-BOOM' motion so I had to time my writing to take my pen off the paper before the 'BOOM'.

The train headed for the large mountains I'd seen in the distance on my ride and all looked very beautiful but bleak. I got my map out and found part of it followed the route I would have taken from Helmsdale to Melvich if the weather had been better. On the whole, I was glad I chose the route from Lazeronwheel.

The girls left at Brora and I strained out of the window, half expecting to see Sally wielding her clubs on the golf course as we passed by.

I was glad to see Lairg albeit briefly – another place I planned to pass through before the weather forced me to change my route. Lairg looked lush with plenty of woodland.

The train then went through Tain and Invergarden before arriving at Dingwall. I looked up from my writing to see the wide sweeping bridge across Cromarty Firth below Culbokie and in a flash it was out of view.

It wasn't long before we arrived at Inverness station at 8.10 pm. I retrieved my bike and bags and tried to get my bearings to make my way to the Youth Hostel.

After 44 miles my legs objected to the final hill up to the Hostel, which was a large modern building around ¾ mile from the station. I booked in and put my bike into their store and then had to go up 2 flights of steps to reach my room – my poor legs! I had a 'micro-room', which was literally a 'cupboard' consisting of a bed and a chair but at least I had it to myself.

The next day, I packed my bags and loaded my bike and was out around 8.45 am. With time to kill, I decided to explore a bit of Inverness and made my way down to the River Ness where I could see the castle. I went over one a footbridge and towards the cathedral, which was disappointingly modern and was only a couple of centuries old.

As I finished reading an information plaque beside the river depicting the castle, I saw a mark on the front tyre of my bike. Swiping my hand across the mark to wipe it off, it was still there. So were several more 'marks' around the tyre. On closer inspection I was horrified to discover the 'marks' were the canvas under the tread of my front tyre! More worrying was the fact that yesterday there was at least one occasion when I was doing over 30 mph on a long descent – the mind boggles at what could have happened if the tyre had blown! I felt most thankful that I had achieved my challenge to complete the ride to John O'Groats without the tyre failing me. I wondered when it had happened – it might have even been whilst riding off-road on the Great Glen Way. I checked my back tyre each morning after it had to be replaced in Fort William but I didn't detect a problem with the front tyre – after all, I could see it in front of me as I rode along. I wonder how long I had 'seen' the problem but not 'seen' it?

Having taken it to my local cycle shop on my return home, the diagnosis was that the tyre had 'perished' rather than worn as there was still plenty of tread – needless to say it has been replaced.

On reflection, I reckon that when I was riding against that dreadful wind on my way to Brora, leaning heavily to the left, I must have put so much strain on the tyre that the tread literally pulled away from it, revealing the canvas below.

I returned to the railway station and found 3 more cyclists there – all waiting for the same train. One of them already had a reservation and made his way onto the train when it came into the correct platform. Another couple had tickets for themselves but not for their bikes. Fully confident, I told them that I had a reservation for both my bike and me to Edinburgh. When it came to the staff checking my tickets, I had tickets for me all the way back to Stourbridge but only had a reservation for my bike from Edinburgh to Stourbridge. The three of us had to wait to speak to the guard to see if she would allow us all on as 'officially' there wouldn't be room for all our bikes. The guard was most understanding and arranged space for us, despite there also being a lady in a wheelchair on the train. The three of us were most relieved and sat together in the carriage.

I learnt my companions were Chris and Audrey from the Lake District. They too had just completed LEJOG, starting from Lands End 3 weeks before and doing the complete ride in one go. They reached John O'Groats on Thursday - the day of the gale-force winds - apparently, it wasn't as ferocious there as it was for me several miles further south. They had a day looking around Orkney on the Friday and then rode to Thurso to catch the train to Inverness on the Saturday morning. Suddenly, the penny dropped – between Castletown and Mey we had crossed each other on the road. I was nearly at John O'Groats and they were heading to Thurso – we'd given each other a cheer and I presumed wrongly that they were just starting their 'JOGLE' (LEJOG the other way round - from north to south).

During the journey to Edinburgh we chatted about our experiences – Audrey doesn't normally ride more than around 30 miles at a time so, with averages of 40-55 miles per day for 3 weeks, she really did a huge achievement. Chris has ridden the Coast-to-Coast several times. Whilst we were chatting, we passed some spectacular scenery, some that they had cycled through and other places where I had been – other places were new to all of us. It brought it home to us how vast and varied Scotland is with the places we passed through including Pitlochry and the Forth Rail and Road Bridges as we entered Edinburgh.

Chris and Audrey left at the first of the two Edinburgh stations and I went on to the terminal at Waverley. As I had a bit of time before my connection so I walked my bike out of the station and was immediately aware that I could smell the exhaust fumes from the trains and traffic. What a difference from the pristine air I had grown accustomed to. I walked to a nearby park full of pleasant spring flowers and I was near the castle but it wasn't quite in view – I could hear someone playing bagpipes too.

I went back to the station and boarded my train to Birmingham New Street. This journey took 6 hours! Thankfully the weather was pleasant and the route started off hugging the coastline. Everywhere was noticeably 'greener' here. Whilst cycling to John O'Groats the trees were only beginning to come into leaf with daffodils and tulips still at their best. At Newcastle I was able to take photos of the bridges as we crossed the River Tyne. The train then passed through Durham, Chesterfield and Sheffield.

I now began to feel pretty travel weary and it was only about 7.00 pm. We continued to travel through Derby and then Tamworth and then arrived at Birmingham New Street.

I got my bike and luggage off the train (as it was continuing to Bristol) but was faced with a flight of steps off the platform. A kind man carried my bike whilst I carried my luggage. Then I had to navigate my way around the station, which had recently been modernised and looked completely different to how I remembered it. It was well signposted and I soon reached Moor Street Station where I took the opportunity to phone Steve whilst I waited for my last train to arrive.

A short journey on the train to Stourbridge and a 2-mile bike ride home from the station, with lights on, and I arrived just before 10.30 pm, making a great fuss of Tinker, my cat – we were both delighted to see each other.

I covered a total of 1088 miles in a total of 25 days and raised £894.00 in sponsorship over the three separate stages for Age UK Dudley's 'Get Cycling for 50 Plus'. I was 59 when I started in 2010 and 62 by the time I finished in 2013.

The whole experience has been awe-inspiring – an adventure of self discovery as well as getting to know my country and meeting such wonderful people along my way.

My challenge was now complete and I feel proud of my achievement. It has aroused a hunger for more adventures in the future. I set out to ride the length of the British Isles to discover the beauty and variety of the landscape along the route.

It was so much more than that. It was the kindness of a friend who laid on lunch for me on my way to Fowey, the unexpected encounter with people I knew at Wells Cathedral, the fascinating and welcoming people who ran the Youth Hostels I stayed in and the B&B's.

It was being able to stay with friends along the route that I hadn't seen for years and sadly the last time I would see my friend Faith before she died.

It was the places of interest I called at such as SS Great Britain at Plymouth, Rob Roy's grave, the magnificence of Dartmoor and Glencoe.

It was the people I met at the places I stayed at where I learned of their own adventures and shared my stories.

It was admiration for the couple along the Caledonian Canal who still managed excursions along the towpath, as the man-made use of an adapted tricycle after suffering a Stroke.

Most of all, it was my chance meeting with Sally Hudson Ross who so kindly allowed me to stay with her in my hour of need when I had to change my route due to appalling weather conditions between Dornoch and Brora. I shall forever be indebted to her and treasure her continuing friendship.

Photos from Stage 3

Monument to King Robert the Bruce at Stirling Castle

Monument to William Wallace – as seen from Stirling Castle

126

Rob Roy's grave at Balquhidder

Viaduct of NCN Route 7 as seen from my route along Glen Ogle

Falls of Dochart at Killin

Snow on mountain tops – Rannach Moor

Clear view of the pass of Glencoe at my picnic stop by River Coe

Towpath along the Caledonian Canal

Loch Ness – 4 miles out of Fort Augustus

Heavy storm approaching – 2 miles from Culbokie

Sally Hudson Ross and Maggie at Brora Bistro – forever grateful to Sally for rescuing me after the scariest bike ride I've ever had in gale-force winds.

Delightful Toremore cottage at Latheron – at one time a B&B – 'Home is where the Heart is'

Sea stacks along the East Coast at Latheronwheel

Dunnet Head from Thurso Beach

Maggie's arrival at John O'Groats

Duncansby Stacks from Duncasnby Head

Shock at the state of my front tyre when I finally noticed the tread had been pulled away from the canvas! The damage was most likely done during the gale-force winds to Brora.

Chapter 11 – Wrapping up and What's Next?

......

Well, it's 7 years since I finished cycling Lands End to John O'Groats and 42 years since I retired from cycle racing and cycling still plays a huge part in my life.

I still regularly clock up 2500 miles cycling each year and once fairly recently managed just over 3000 miles in one year. During my cycle racing days I would clock up between 5000 and 6000 miles!

My partner, Steve and I have had some wonderful cycling holidays. In 2014 we did some car-assisted cycling in Scotland, retracing parts of my route to John O'Groats the year before and called to visit Sally again. On our return, we drove along part of the route Steve rode in 1997 when he cycled the 'JOGLE' – John O'Groats to Lands End then other way round. Magnificent mountain scenery.

In 2015 we rode a tour of East Anglia, taking the train to Peterborough, then staying in Spalding where I lived from 1958 to 1961. We even paid a visit to my old home – 'Hollandia House' and were invited in by the present occupiers. Also we visited my old school at Ayscoughfee Hall ... such nostalgia. Well and truly in The Fens, we were grateful for tailwinds to Kings Lynn and a visit to Castle Acre on our way to stay with Steve's cousin Matthew and his wife Helen near North Elmham. We stayed a night at Bury St Edmunds where my Dad was born and where he and my Mum met. Our route took us through the picturesque village of Lavenham and we stayed at the home of my aunt Barbara at Ferneux Pelham, whose husband had been my Godfather. Then it was a mad dash to catch the train back from Stanstead.

Another challenge in 2016 – Mont Ventoux! Having watched the Tour de France climb this 'monster' many times on TV, I wanted to see if I could conquer it. This was a car-assisted holiday and we camped at the foot of the mountain at a lovely place called Villes Sur Auzon. To say that I had underestimated the difficulty of riding up this mountain is an under-statement and I clearly wasn't fit enough. Thinking that the overall gradient was around 8% I felt this was manageable. The reality was that it was nearer 10% up to Chalet Reynard (which is about two-thirds of the way up) and the last section around 7.5 %. For kilometre after kilometre the road snaked through the woodland, which was a blessing as it was a hot day at the start. But it was relentless. I was doing around 3.5 to 4 mph maximum in my lowest gear. Unlike Alpe d'Huez that has 21 hairpin bends along its ascent, there was just one hairpin … without a flat section on the bend. I was relieved that Steve passed me frequently in the car and we stopped at Chalet Reynard for a well-deserved rest and lunch before riding the last couple of miles. Steve joined me for this section too. We passed the memorial to Tom Simpson who died in the 1967 Tour de France on this climb and just before the top the weather changed to become quite stormy and very windy. At one point it wasn't safe to ride along the top ridge, so I walked for about 100 metres and we both made it to the top in a howling gale. We needed winter clothes and gloves to descend back to Chalet Reynard and our car. It certainly lived up to its name – Windy Mountain.

In 2017 we had our wettest cycle tour – in northern France. We arrived on a beautiful balmy summer day – the channel crossing had been like a millpond. During the night we were woken by a thunderstorm and our first day was a very soggy ride to Cassel, near the border with Belgium. Taking our hands out of soggy gloves at the end of the day's ride, our hands looked all mottled like we'd been in a bath all day. Next day was a complete contrast and we had a pleasurable ride to Ypres and the Menin Gate – a very moving and somber visit. Taking the train from Lille to Arras, we cycled to the town of Albert with more memorials to WW1. We were able to ride alongside the River Somme to Amiens passing 'Les Hortillonages', which is a market gardening area served by a picturesque narrow canal system. Our next stop was Beauvais – full of medieval history. We were then on our homeward stretch and stayed at the Youth Hostel at the town of Eu. William the Conquerer married Matilda in this town in 1050. On another very wet day we cycled through Ault, which had a dramatic coastline where we had an absolute drenching, and then through Crecy – this was THE Crecy from the Hundred Year's War between King Edward 111 of England and King Phillip of France. The next two places were Montreuil Sur Mer and finally Guines before taking the ferry back home.

Another challenge for 2018 – this time using hired mountain bikes. Steve and I have both watched the film 'The Way' several times. It stars Martin Sheen as a father who walks the pilgrim route from St Jean Pied de Port in France to Santiago de Compostela in Spain – the pilgrim walk that his son planned to do. The scenery was spectacular and we decided to cycle part of the route from Leon in Castile, which covered around 300 kms of the route. The overwhelming feeling from this ride was the camaraderie amongst all who travelled the route – mostly walkers but several on bikes too. Everyone shouted 'Buen Camino' to each other. The terrain was mixed with some minor roads and often stony tracks – hence using mountain bikes. For a large part of the last 100 kms, we used tracks, sharing them with a lot of walkers. There were 'pilgrims' undertaking this route from many different countries – it often felt as though we were traveling with the 'world' in the most amicable of circumstances. The long climb up to Cruz de Ferro was a memorable experience as there is a massive 'cairn' of stones and pebbles against a very tall iron cross at the top of the climb. People that undertake this journey traditionally take a stone from their home to leave at this cairn for a special reason – to remember someone or a cherished memory. The cairn stood about 8 feet tall having been built over many centuries by travelers. Reading some of the messages it was a very moving experience. The next highlight was the climb up to El Cebriero – a tiny hamlet in the mountains of Galicia. We approached it with about 10 kilometres to go at the end of the day and the gradient of the climb reminded me of Mont Ventoux. It was a very hot afternoon with little shade and it soon became clear we would end up walking up the climb. It still took us over 2 hours to climb. The scenery was beautiful and when we stopped to look back the way we had come, the view was stunning. It was a highlight of the whole journey. As we approached Santiago de Compostela, we reached Mont de Gozo and from here we had a fantastic vista of the city and the spires of the cathedral. There were some sculptures of ancient pilgrims looking and pointing towards the cathedral just 5 kms away. Our journey ended at an office in the city where we were able to gain our certificate of completion, which we are both very proud of.

Next was a cycle tour nearer home. In May 2019 we took the ferry with our bikes to the Isle of Man with the intention of cycling around the whole island. What a most delightful place … home from home and feeling as though we were in a bit of a time warp … like the 1960's. Setting off from Douglas we cycled to Laxey where there is an amazing water wheel – a remnant from the Industrial Revolution when it powered the zinc mine in the area. It is now a tourist spot and was fascinating to look around. We took a tram to the top of Snaefell, the highest mountain on the island, setting off in a thick mist and delighted when it lifted so we could enjoy the views from the top. Next we rode through Ramsey to the far north of the island – the Point of Ayre before returning to our accommodation for a second night. On leaving the next day, we stopped to look at a Neolithic stone circle from around 1800 BC. Our next destination was Peel and part of our route was along a disused railway line. There was a huge castle and cathedral ruin at Peel and also a fascinating museum telling the turbulent history of the town including visits from Viking armies. We continued our journey to Castletown on the south end of the island and this is where the original parliament called 'Tynwald' was sited, as the Isle of Man is independent of UK government. A bit further on was Port Erin and Milner's Tower – from the tower we could see the 'Calf of Man' the true southern end of the Isle. We had a very hilly ride to Cregneash where we found another Neolithic stone circle. Returning to Castletown we did our final ride back to Douglas, riding along the picturesque Marine Drive that is closed to traffic as there had been a landslide but is open to cyclists, horse riders and walkers. The geology here is incredible and reminded me of Lulworth

Cove as the striations of rock twist and turn in all directions having been warped by earth movements millennia earlier. It was along this last few miles that we cycled by a couple of photographers and, curiosity getting the better of us, we asked them what they were taking photos of. There was a Peregrin Falcon's nest with three chicks.

As I am now reaching the end of this book in 2020, the world has been shaken by the COVID 19 pandemic since the last week of March. Steve and I had planned a cycle tour to Northern Ireland with a visit to the Giant's Causeway as part of our route. This has been put 'on the shelf' for the time being to be picked up again once we have freedom of movement and social distancing has been lifted.

The 'Lockdown' has given me the opportunity to finish this book and to reflect on the wonderful adventures I have had whilst travelling self-propelled on two wheels. The places I've seen, the scent and sounds of different places, the familiarity of others. Being able to share these cycling experiences with Steve has been a delight along with all the amazing people we have met on our travels.

What next? Northern Ireland soon hopefully. We both long to return to France again … for the variety, food and wine and also a place where cycling is the norm, as it is also in the Netherlands. There are plenty of places in England, Wales and Scotland that we would like to do more cycling in too. Watch this space …..

I have made references to Laughter Yoga several times within this book and it has become my second passion after cycling. It is a combination of laughter exercises, hand claps and deep breathing with eye contact and childlike playfulness. I first came across it in 2009 and loved it so much that I trained to become a Leader and later to become a Teacher. Running four Laughter Yoga clubs a month locally and also for different organisations, it has become my retirement 'career' as I have run it as a small business since 2014. I laugh every day, many times for around 15-minutes at a time and I feel joyful and uplifted by it, knowing it is helping me keep my immune system healthy. I absolutely love doing it with other people, as I see the difference it makes to their health and wellbeing when they have taken part in it. Quite often people attend my Laughter Yoga clubs and are clearly apprehensive as I guide them through exercises and breathing that takes them out of their comfort zones. By the end of the session they are clearly jubilant with huge smiles on their faces and sparkling eyes, having made deep connections with other participants.

Acknowledgements

I am hugely indebted to my sister, Pat Gordon-Smith, who has helped me to create this book through her editing skills. Without her advice and patience I doubt it would ever have been completed.

One of the first things she asked me was who am I addressing in my book? I am primarily writing it for my sons and grandchildren … so they understand a bit more about this crazy Mum and Grandmother that rides a bicycle. There are other family references in the book linked to extended family too.

Pat helped me to edit out the inconsequential and mundane things and concentrate on bringing my personality and passion into my experiences. She has guided me to bring my racing experiences into the book as I originally only intended it to be about my Lands End to John O'Groats adventure.

When I first sent her some drafts she provided the helpful critic that it read like a diary entry and would soon bore most readers. Learning this lesson has enabled me to write what I hope will be an engaging read through the ups and downs of my racing career interspersed with the three separate stages of my Lands End to John O'Groats ride. Pat encouraged me to write about what I felt as though I was telling a friend about my experiences so that it conveyed my passion. I hope this is what I convey and shall be forever grateful to Pat for her expertise.

I would also like to thank Andy Thompson, my ex-husband, for his patience and belief in me during my racing career – I could not have achieved my Championship titles without him.

I would like to thank my sons Alex Thompson and Vincent Thompson who have enriched my life through their childhood. I feel so proud of them and the wonderful young men they have become, along with their families.

Finally, I thank Steve Glennie-Smith for all the amazing cycling holidays and generally days out on two wheels since we met by chance on the Sea-Cat ferry from Poole to St Malo on independent solo cycle tours in 2001.